I0801741

DUE SANTI

and the

UNIVERSITY OF DALLAS

Un Piccolo Paradiso

EDITED BY GREGORY ROPER AND ANDREW MORAN

FOREWORD BY THOMAS HIBBS

THE History PRESS

Published by The History Press
Charleston, SC
www.historypress.com

Front cover image courtesy of Michael Housewright. Back cover images: Top: Jim Fougerousse at the beginning, with Sister Georgianne Segner, SSND. *Rome Campus Archives*. Bottom: The First Romers. *University of Dallas Archives*.

First published 2020

Manufactured in the United States

ISBN 9781467147651

Library of Congress Control Number: 2020938434

DUE SANTI

and the

UNIVERSITY OF DALLAS

CONTENTS

Contents

FOREWORD

Like Saint John Henry Newman, who took a Mediterranean journey at a pivotal moment in his own life's journey, University of Dallas students have for half a century been traveling to Rome at a crucial period in their own intellectual, moral, and spiritual development. As do our faculty and students, Newman sought to encounter in an intimate way the settings of the stories that had informed his own education. He read the *Odyssey* at the age of ten (!), as well as the *Aeneid* and the *Divine Comedy*—texts that anchor the university's core curriculum. Newman also identified a danger for travelers: the impressions of travel, "like the shifting scenes of a show," can "leave the spectator where he was." In education, as in life, we can be mere tourists.

The UD Rome semester counters the tourist temptation through its commitment both to a rigorous curriculum and to a communal life characterized by thought and prayer, conversation and study. The other corrective has to do with the university's anchoring of its program in a particular place, Due Santi.

The current volume explores the *genius loci* of the Eugene Constantin Rome Campus in the Castelli Romani, south of Rome, with its ancient and modern history. The history has become part of the University of Dallas, and now the university—its curriculum, mores, students, faculty, and staff—has become woven into the history of the place.

My hope is that this fine book will be an occasion for a deepening of the collective memory of the University of Dallas and for expressions of gratitude for a place, a curriculum, and a community of teachers and students. The Due Santi campus has always sought renewal through a return to the roots of things, the foundations of classical and Christian civilization that owe so much to Rome.

Thomas Hibbs, President

ACKNOWLEDGEMENTS

After hearing me talk about the Piga family, the villa, and its connection to Italian history, Brad Blue, my Rome colleague in 2008–9, said I should "drop everything and write this up." He gave me the impetus to start interviewing the Pigas and to conceive of a history of Due Santi that would include their family and UD. To Brad goes the first thanks.

The Piga family—especially Guglielmo; Dario; Gabriella; Gustavo and his wife, Patricia Thomas; and Nicole Dunaway—have been most generous with their time, coming to campus to be interviewed, opening their homes to me, and allowing me to hear stories, happy and painful, from the past. Their generosity in sharing their family home with UD is heartening and their joy at seeing it a living campus palpable. This book could not exist without them, and I hope it brings them joy to see their family home of many decades recounted, praised, and loved as they loved it.

As the anniversaries of the Rome Program and the Due Santi campus grew closer, I realized that other duties meant that I could not write the entire book myself. I decided to invite others to contribute chapters, and you see here the benefit of that choice. To Wayne Ambler, Peter Hatlie, Danny Milligan, Andrew Moran, Val Hrbacek, Silvia De Simone, Michael Housewright, Lyle Novinski, and Lisa Mobus, a grand thank you; you have contributed so much more than I envisioned possible through my own efforts.

Special thanks are also due to Acquisitions Editor Ben Gibson (Spring Romer, 2004, UD English BA, 2006) at The History Press. I ran into Ben at Groundhog and told him of the then-floundering project. He thought the idea wonderful, did not want it to die, and went beyond his professional responsibilities to get it published. Thanks to

Acknowledgements

Ryan Finn and the other editors and designers at The History Press for producing the beautiful book you hold in your hands.

Thanks also to Shelley Gayler-Smith, archivist at the University of Dallas Blakely-Cowan Library, who gave us access to a treasure-trove of documents and images about the UD Rome Program; to Peter Hatlie, for another treasure-trove, including back issues of *Forum Romanum*, the Rome Campus newsletter (www.udallas.edu/rome/romecampus/romecampusnews.php); and to Jason Wu Trujillo, vice-president of advancement, and his staff, especially Sarah Oates. Through the information, stories, and insights of those who allowed us to interview them—the late Bob Sasseen, Brian Whalen, Randy and Lisa Irlbeck, Lyle and Sybil Novinski, and Wayne Ambler—this book has been possible. And the photographers have made it beautiful; thanks to all of you, alumni, staff, and students, especially to Vasile Chiriac, Stephen Henderson, and Michael Housewright.

The profits from this book will fund the Charles T. Uhl Memorial Scholarship, which helps students defray the cost of attending the program. Danny and Kathy Milligan, with her family, founded the scholarship and have supported this book from the beginning.

Thanks also go to my family, who after being uprooted and taken to Rome have endured the many hours I gave to the book instead of them.

Gregory Roper,
on behalf of Andrew Moran

INTRODUCTION

FROM THE OLD ROME CAMPUS TO THE NEW

WAYNE AMBLER

I was fortunate and honored to have taught in the University of Dallas Rome Program for ten years and am honored again to introduce this volume celebrating the fiftieth anniversary of the program. I was invited to do so, I'm told, because I was present during the last year of the main old campus at Via del Pescaccio in 1988–89 and present again at the opening of the new campus at Due Santi in 1994. Oddly, my family and I also ended up living on the new campus before it became a campus, in 1989–90, when it was a once elegant but then run-down country villa. The official (temporary) campus was then in Vitinia, a forty-minute drive. I'm therefore in a good position to speak of campuses both old and new.

Few things are as obvious as the differences between them. At Via del Pescaccio, there was very limited space for outdoor activities—just a table and a few chairs on a strip of grass. Internal space for gathering was also in short supply, and there was no library to speak of. My wife and I and our two daughters shared a bedroom so small we had to fold up a cot in order to move about during the day, and we gave the kids their baths in a laundry tub. The ceiling in the kitchen was so low we couldn't stand up straight, so we had no choice but to watch the pot while the pasta water boiled. We had rats on our balcony, and the Frank family had one in their kitchen. Eventually, in a dramatic encounter, we menfolk solved at least that problem, with Randy Irlbeck using a mallet to deliver the *coup de grâce* while I immobilized the critter by pinning its tail to the ground with a squeegee.

Alitalia
NEIL ARMSTRONG
Alitalia

OPPOSITE, TOP
The first Romers, Fall 1970 (as evidenced by the bell bottoms), prepare to embark on Alitalia's "Neil Armstrong." *University of Dallas Archives.*

OPPOSITE, BOTTOM
Early Romers at Via del Pescaccio submit to a group photograph; the ruins of Mussolini's mistress's palazzo beckon from behind. *Rome Campus Archives.*

LEFT
A view down the side of Via del Pescaccio's three "towers." *Rome Campus Archives.*

Nor were there any little towns nearby, like the charming Castelli towns among which Due Santi is nestled. We did not have to tell the students to leave the campus and go to Rome—they had no alternative, save for some filthy ruins and an old bar or two.

Since the campus has now been at Due Santi for more than twenty-five years, most of you are familiar with it, and a shortlist of a few of its marvels can replace an adequate description. It features a vineyard, more than one hundred olive trees, a swimming pool and tennis court, a wonderful outdoor *forno* and patio under live oaks and umbrella pines, athletic fields, Teatro Due Santi (improperly called "the amphitheater"), an attractive dining room and patio, a capacious classroom, and a library. You all know: it's extraordinary! What else would you expect, moving campus from "the Street of the Rotten Fish" to the meeting place of Saints Peter and Paul?

So it's true, the move from Via del Pescaccio to Due Santi, by way of two interim campuses, was a

"Oh, how happy I am in Rome…. / The night shines bright with stars, echoes with gentle song, / And the Moon shines clearer to me than Northern day" (Goethe, "Roman Elegies"). *Vasile Chiriac.*

jump from a dump to paradise. But to leave it at this is to get it all wrong. Although the setting of the Rome Program changed radically, and certainly changed for the better, the program itself was and is extraordinary in both locations. There was still that wonderful curriculum back at the old campus, the same remarkable spirit among students and faculty, and the same enthusiasm for mixing the excitement of travel and learning. I love Due Santi and will now boast shamelessly of having had the bright idea to plant the strip of grass and roses that divides the vineyard, as well as actually planting those roses with the help of Luke Speier, Terry Landry, Vincenzo, and Fabio. But my year teaching at Via del Pescaccio was also wonderful, in spite of the cramped quarters. As for the rats, the director of the program at the time, Jim Fougerousse, made light of them by calling them "wire-tailed Apennine squirrels," and so we did with other such inconveniences. It is the Rome Program that is most important, roses or not.

Why? The Rome Program does not represent all of UD's excellences. It does not offer, for example, strong programs in a variety of major fields, a top-notch pre-med program, intercollegiate athletics, or a most unusual and admirable Institute of Philosophic Studies. But it does embody UD's core curriculum, which is a big part of what makes the Irving campus a wonderful place to teach and learn. Rome and Irving are both radical to the core, even if they look conservative in the eyes of the world. If we unpack the core and look inside it, what we find are fundamental ideas with far-reaching consequences—and, thank goodness, these ideas are discordant. They represent diversity at its finest and most necessary. If all the readings in the core repeated the same ideas, it might be reduced to a single book. As matters stand, however, such an attempt would provoke a battle royal over what this book should be! Would it be the Bible, Aristotle's *Ethics*, Dante's *Divine Comedy*, or Nietzsche's *Beyond Good and Evil*? Who would say that these books all agree and hence do not require readers to think about their differences and relative merits?

Like the core in general, the Rome Program incarnates the excellence of bringing to the fore a battleground of competing ideas. Not only do students and faculty confront them in the classroom, but they also become visible in visits to sites that bring to life alternatives represented by Ancient Greece and Rome, Christian Rome, Medieval Assisi, Renaissance Florence, and the Modern West in general.

Andrew Moran will have more to say about the curriculum, so I will return to my subject, that of the different campuses, but it is imperative to keep the campuses in their place. One is much more beautiful and comfortable than all the others, but—at least in my view—none of them outshines the education they exist to serve.

Its beauty apart, the Due Santi Campus also brings real educational advantages. Dean Peter Hatlie has continued to improve the library, and the campus as a whole has many good places to study and exchange ideas. This is good! The Aula Magna and Teatro Due Santi are both wonderful places for lectures, and the latter has been used to put on some remarkably good plays, thanks to such talented students, in my day, as Dan Forsythe, Teresa Danze, Kyle Lemieux, Jon Bird, and Peter Heyne. Improved faculty living conditions for families have made it more possible to attract good faculty from Irving. This means better classes in Rome, but returning Rome faculty then also share in Irving what they learned in Rome. The athletic fields offer an opportunity for pleasant and healthy diversions and further exchanges between faculty and students. Good meals in an attractive *mensa* also draw faculty into opportunities to mingle with students, whereas, well, this was not the case at Via del Pescaccio.

I was asked about the transition from the old campuses to the new one at Due Santi. My involvement is limited to two "moments" in this period. One was in 1989–90, when my family—including future Rome assistant Sara Ambler, then a newborn Roman baby—lived in not-so-splendid isolation at the villa that would later be part of the Due Santi Campus. There was no room for us at the Vitinia Campus, but the Piga family, who were selling their villa to the university, kindly agreed to let us stay there, perhaps thinking that the transaction would proceed smoothly, as it did not. It probably sounds wonderful to think of life in the Italian countryside in a twenty-room villa, and it was, but bear these details in mind: The villa had not been occupied for years. There was thick dust on everything. The clothes, and wigs (!), of deceased family members were still in the closets. There was initially no heat. (A certain Giorgio, Vincenzo, and I installed a new heater.) Water came from a toilet bowl–like basin in the attic accessible to pigeons, so I went to a fountain to fill bottles for our drinking water. There were no English speakers for miles around, and our Italian was not good. There was no gate to the property, and we once encountered Romani (*i Zingari*) in our bedroom; on another occasions, we could tell they had visited, but our paths did not cross. I got good at disabling bats in our bedroom with my tennis racket.

But there were also Adele and Vincenzo, the property's Italian caretakers, who also took care of us. We went with them to Mass in the charming Bernini church in Castel Gandolfo, and they introduced us to the butcher, several bakers, and the pasta lady. They invited us to their very informal dinner parties, which featured simple country dishes, sometimes including birds that they raised along with their chickens. A few such gatherings included dancing: my wife did the tango with Piero, he with a rose stem in his teeth; I preferred simpler steps with children, who were wonderfully non-judgmental. Vincenzo and I made wine, perhaps the world's most unsanitary ever, and grappa, which seems not to have affected my vision. He spoke to me of World War II, when in 1943–44 the Nazis occupied the

Wayne Ambler uses the authority of his Zeus-like forehand to preside over the Greek Olympics. *Wayne Ambler.*

villa and American troops were shelling the area from their bridgehead at Anzio. He was most animated in describing the thrill of seeing American motorcycles, trucks, and tanks streaming down the Via Appia en route to Rome, which they liberated the day before D-Day.

We tried to reciprocate as best we could, but we did not always know what they might enjoy. My wife made a delicious basil pesto, for example, of which Vincenzo said, "*Ma e' verde*," which did not seem to be a compliment. I took it as a reminder that his life as a simple *contadino* had not allowed him all the pleasant variety Italian food has to offer. But our Thanksgiving dinner in 1989 was a rip-roaring success, an abundant offering served in a single course and without pasta, two near-miracles in the eyes of our Italian guests. It was a challenge to find a farm that would sell me a whole turkey, and when I ordered it, the farmer's wife asked me, "*Vivo o morto?*" I responded, "*Morto ma pulito.*" She disappeared for fifteen minutes and then handed me a bird that was certainly *morto*, but its temperature felt to be about 98.6 when she handed it over. It came complete with various internal parts I was not expecting.

Meanwhile, I commuted to Vitinia to teach, but my wife had a rougher bargain, having to take care of three children with precious little help or mature company. The winter was long, cold, wet, and dark.

The other transition of which I had a little experience was the opening of the Due Santi Campus, which involved a week of the classic UD mix of education and partying. From June 4 to June 11, 1994, the university sponsored what got called "The World Class in Rome and Assisi," and we tried to show members of the board and other donors what a UD education in Rome was like. So, for a week, various UD faculty led discussions of readings from Virgil, Shakespeare, Plato, and Saints Benedict and Thomas, and from works on Catholic liberal arts education, including Pope John Paul II's *Ex Corde Ecclesiae*. We combined the discussions with trips to Rome, Assisi, and Monte Cassino. Not only had Saint Benedict built his main and Europe-changing monastery there, but it was also at Cassino that the Germans had anchored their Gustav Line and blocked the Allies' march north during World War II. Our "World Class" occurred on the fiftieth anniversary of the breakthrough at Cassino that led directly to the liberation of Rome. We did not know, when we planned it, that the chair of the board had served in the Italian campaign during the war, but he seemed especially moved by the visit to a site of such crucial importance for the war and for him personally. Once we got past the liberation of Rome, all the dignitaries gathered, and we had one hell of a party. Due Santi got off to a great start, and it is a tremendous satisfaction to see how well the campus has fulfilled its purpose in serving the program.

CHAPTER 1

THE ANCIENT ROMAN CITY OF BOVILLAE

History Just Below Our Feet

PETER HATLIE

Among the many benefits that the University of Dallas Eugene Constantin Rome Campus offers its residents and visitors is a precious and very human window into the past. Greece, Rome, and the many historic cities of Italy are naturally more famous for their capacity to raise our awareness and deepen our knowledge of the history of Western civilization and our place in it. Yet don't count out the Rome Campus in this regard either. Whereas our acquaintance with more famous places such as Delphi, Athens, Rome, and Florence is occasional and brief, the historical voice that speaks to us on the Rome Campus is constant, quietly insistent, and often very personal. It would be no exaggeration to say that we embrace, internalize, and get very close to inhabiting a profound spirit and appreciation of the past—at many different levels—on the Rome Campus. This is one of the many reasons why a sojourn in Rome can be a marvelous, even life-changing experience. When it comes time to leave the Rome Campus, there is always a certain feeling that we have gained a better and indeed privileged perspective on who we are, where we came from, and possibly where we are going as the result of walking in the footsteps and hearing the distant echoes of the voices of those who came before us. History, in sum, comes alive and carries weight on the Rome Campus.

The historical journey of the Rome Program begins with the neighborhood around campus, named "Due Santi" in recognition of long-standing local memories of Rome's two greatest saints, Saint Peter and Saint Paul. Like the thousands of Christian pilgrims and saints who followed in their footsteps over the centuries, Peter and Paul walked to Rome via the Appian Way, the great old Roman road or "Queen of Roads" (*regina viarum*) that passes right under our feet. The historical journey of UD Rome continues with the particular pace, contours, and traditions of life on the campus itself—from the old-world food and homegrown wine on offer to the relative slowness of life, the prominence given to cultivation of the Catholic faith, and UD's serious commitment to a classical education. Sometimes the campus feels as much at home in the medieval world in these respects as it does in modern times. Not least of UD Rome's windows into the past are its landscapes. The campus grounds are not just beautiful and full of grace. Even the most casual visitor will remark how ancient and somehow venerable the knolls, slopes, valleys, and outlooks of campus seem to be, as though this landscape has watched centuries of time pass it by, as though this very landscape was meant for this very place, and as though some great treasure lies below the ground.

All these qualities of the Rome Campus are beyond dispute to anyone who has lived here. Anyone who lives here for any time whatsoever comes to sense this historical dimension as one among so many wonderful things that animate life on campus. As it turns out, too, the UD Rome Campus can also make an objective claim to being a site of considerable historical importance in its own right. And the more we learn about this aspect of the campus's historical background—namely, that an ancient city lies below our feet—the more exciting and meaningful the historical dimension of campus gets.

UD Rome sits on top of a prominent ancient city called Bovillae. More specifically, its vineyard and buildings occupy a space that ancient Bovilliaeans would have identified as the southeastern corner of their city—a neighborhood located just inside the city walls, near a city gate leading to the Appian Way and known to people far and wide for its large chariot racing stadium, an important religious complex dedicated to the family of Julius Caesar, and the bubbling waters of its impressive nymphaeum (or monumental water fountain). To imagine Bovillae as it was in its heyday, we should imagine a well-heeled suburb of the modern day, located on the outskirts of a major metropolitan center, proud of its own history and heritage and yet clearly drawing on the wealth and contacts of the bigger city on which it was dependent.

Remains of the ancient city of Bovillae are today almost invisible to the eye, even though it can be identified as one of the earliest Latin cities to emerge in prehistoric times (circa 800 BC) and later became one of ancient Rome's most important suburbs during the two centuries between the age of Julius Caesar and the end of Rome's Julio-Claudian dynasty of emperors (circa 100 BC–AD 100). The fate of Bovillae attracted the keen attention of scholars, travelers, and treasure hunters of the nineteenth and early twentieth centuries. Oddly, though, it has only been of marginal interest since then. Several recent finds in the area have, however, put Bovillae back into the limelight. One of these, an exquisite first-century marble bust of the emperor Titus (AD 79–81), was found about a mile from campus in the year 2012 and was on loan to UD Rome for public display. In addition to this spectacular recent find, archaeological research

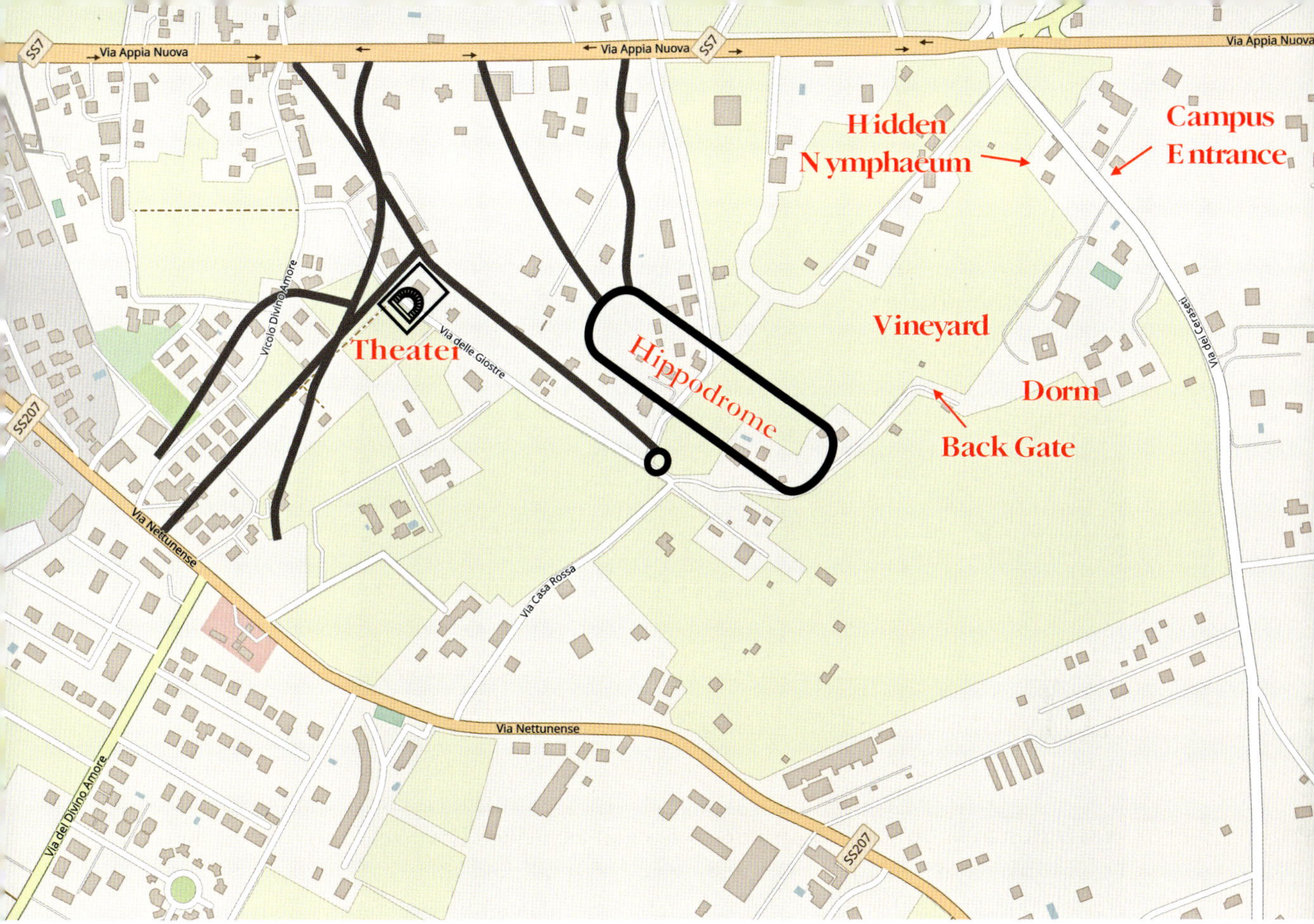

Map of ancient Bovillae, showing the present campus in relation to the hippodrome and theater. *Map data@ OpenStreetMap contributors; overlay Gabriel Roper.*

in the area has recovered as many as 1,600 artifacts from ancient Bovillae over the last five years. These and other findings came to light in a major international conference hosted by the University of Dallas Rome Campus in May 2015, a conference that has energized a pro-Bovillae movement in the local community.

The population of Bovillae must have numbered in the hundreds or even thousands by around 500 BC, and by circa AD 100, it had grown well beyond that point in both numbers and importance. Among the reasons for its ascent was that it came to serve as site of memory for the family of Emperor Augustus and his adoptive great-uncle, Julius Caesar. After Augustus's death at Nola in southern Italy, his body lay in state at Bovillae for a time before being brought to Rome for funeral ceremonies. An important shrine to the Julian line was erected there shortly afterward, reminding Romans not only of these two imposing figures in recent political history but also of the divinely born royal family—going all the way back to Aeneas and the goddess

Bust of the Emperor Titus, on loan from the *Soprintendenza Archeologia del Lazio e dell'Etruria Meridionale*. *Stephen Henderson*.

Venus—that had produced them and, to some degree, Rome itself. The city's particularly close ties to the memory of the divinized Caesar (100–44 BC) and the subsequent Julio-Claudian line of Roman emperors (AD 27–68) gave Bovillae a preeminent status among the Latin cities of the time. Further proof of its elevated status during this age is to be found in a famous map of the first century AD. A marvelous thirteenth-century AD copy of that map called the *Tabula Peutingeriana* is still preserved, and it pictures "Bobellas" (an alternative spelling to Bovillae) as the biggest city in the hinterland of Rome. Bovillae is flagged on the map by an imposing three-roomed inn, which was located at the entrance to the city and was its chief calling card back then, something similar to the great Gateway Arch in St. Louis or the Statue of Liberty in New York. That same inn is incorporated within a structure combining a hardware store, bakery, and bar today.

Written sources confirm Bovillae's ancient origins and highlight particular moments of notoriety. One of these, the so-called *Origin of the Roman People*, places it among the top ten cities of early Latin people. Along with Rome, it was subordinate to Alba Longa, the city founded by Aeneas's son Ascanius, located just up the hill from Bovillae. Several colorful stories about ancient Bovillae from later centuries emerge in other sources. Ovid traced the worship of the local Roman goddess Anna Perenna to an old woman from Bovillae whose beneficence in a time of scarcity and trial in Rome left people so much in awe that they erected a holy shrine to her. Cicero recounted the details of an infamous brawl that took place at a tavern in Bovillae—the architectural core of which still stands today—leaving one of his political enemies, Clodius, dead at the hands of a rival politician and gangster named Milo. Ancient epigraphy reveals that the city hosted an important school of theater. Indeed, Rome's most famous actor of the second century AD, a certain mime by the name of Acilius, apparently worked out of Bovillae.

Plunderers and treasure hunters from the last days of Rome through the nineteenth century have displaced or removed all major physical remains of ancient Bovillae. Parts of a monumental stone relief depicting scenes from the *Iliad* and once displayed in Bovillae, called the *Tabula Iliaca Capitolina*, are now to be found in Rome's Capitoline Museums. Beautiful statues of both the god Dionysus and an anonymous noblewoman (or goddess) are housed nearby at Rome's Palazzo Massimo Museum. Artifacts from Bovillae have also made their way to locations farther away, including a priceless relief called the *Apotheosis of Homer*, attributed to the famous Hellenistic sculptor Archaelaus of Priene (circa 300 BC), now found in the British Museum. In addition, a statue of the Emperor Caligula is now owned by the Richmond, Virginia Museum of Art.

The fate of other impressive finds, known only through the personal papers of various buyers and sellers, is difficult to trace. Around the year 1800, for example, two huge statues found at Bovillae, each reportedly thirty feet tall, were sold to a notorious Irish treasure hunter, broker, and painter by the name of Robert Fagan, never to resurface in a private collection or museum again, in part because of his later money troubles and suicide. Curiously enough, the legs of one of the most famous Roman copies of a Greek statue ever produced also came from Bovillae. Created in the late third century BC, it is today called the *Farnese Hercules* and can be found at the Naples Archaeological Museum, complete with two sets of legs—the artificial ones made by the Renaissance sculptor Guglielmo della Porta while Hercules's original legs still lay in the ground, and the rediscovered legs that were finally reunited with their owner after being found in Bovillae.

Looking out upon UD Rome's slice of ancient Bovillae today, one can be forgiven for failing to notice and appreciate its existing visible remains. For one thing, UD Rome's buildings and grounds cover the ancient streets, houses, and shops that, whatever their current state of preservation, once constituted the brick and mortar of this neighborhood. For another, the soft and easy beauty of UD Rome's landscape can distract attention from what few physical remains are still visible at ground level. The road leading to and from campus, *Via dei Ceraseti*, follows the path of the old city wall, pierced by an old city gate just up the road. Several ancient marble and stone blocks, some with epigraphy and decoration, lie here and there around the UD campus—one block near the swimming pool, a road marker near the tennis court, and others near the villa, along with a pile of stone water channels and other cut stone blocks to be found beyond the vineyard. Within the vineyard itself there is an archaeological ruin called "the cistern," which is probably not a cistern at all but rather an extension of Bovillae's impressive nymphaeum (or "grand fountain") complex. Although never fully excavated, it is not hard to imagine that this nymphaeum complex had its origins somewhere up on the hill between campus and the nearby town of Castel Gandolfo, and from there the water cascaded its way downward to and through our campus vineyard through numerous water channels that varied its pace and visual effects along the way. Where there are Roman nymphaeums there are also figurative statues, other types of lavish architectural sculptural decoration, and probably mosaics. Mosaics were reported to have been uncovered in the vineyard and then assiduously covered over again by UD Rome's

OPPOSITE, TOP
"This masonry is wondrous; fates broke it; / Courtyards were smashed, the work of giants is decaying" (Anglo-Saxon, "The Ruin"). *Vasile Chiriac.*

OPPOSITE, BOTTOM
The "cistern" from Bovillae's nymphaeum. *Michael Housewright.*

beloved caretaker and gardener around the year AD 2000. Some of the prestigious sculpture that has found its way to the great museums in Rome and elsewhere may have come from this area right around the campus vineyard too.

Modern archaeologists staged several campaigns in Bovillae, including in the area around the current location of our campus, toward the end of the nineteenth and beginning of the twentieth centuries. These were not archaeological excavations as such, but rather surveys of known monuments, including remains of the nymphaeum complex just noted, interspersed with whatever scattered materials had come to light. Among the most important results of these campaigns was the discovery of the location of downtown Bovillae, which appears to have been about two hundred yards from the UD campus. This downtown area consisted of, at a minimum, a forum, a theater, a temple or two, a prominent shrine to the Julian family, and an important chariot-racing stadium, or circus. Suburban expansion and illegal building in recent decades have robbed us of all of these buildings except parts of the still impressive stadium. The *carceres* or starting blocks of this first-century AD stadium, built by the emperor Tiberius in honor of the Julian family, still stand today. Recent research has suggested that it served as a stadium of champions—some rough equivalent to the All-Star or Pro-Bowl nominees of today—for the Roman emperors and people of the first century AD. The anniversary of any Julian emperor featured chariot races and religious ceremonies to honor them. A college of priests called the *sodales augustales*, who had a prominent meeting hall in Bovillae and were responsible for managing imperial cult matters, presided over these affairs. One of the highlights of such anniversaries was the spectacle of having Rome's finest and fiercest chariot riders square off against one another in a race of elites. That's what the remarkable stadium of Bovillae was built and served for throughout the first century and perhaps beyond.

As painful as it may be to say, Bovillae's decline and demise is indirectly tied up with UD Rome's great fortune in buying and developing the property on which its wonderful Rome Campus today lies. Bovillae had practically disappeared by the end of the Middle Ages. Not only were its streets and buildings largely destroyed or buried by circa AD 1500, but even its name also came to be forgotten and then replaced over time by the name of the small village of Frattocchie (translated as "uncultivated lands") that lay on top of it. Over time, the city was stripped of its wealth, livelihood, and heritage. Eventually, small manors and small farms came to dominate the local landscape, one of which finally passed to the Piga family in the 1930s and then ultimately was acquired by UD Rome in 1990 and developed in the years 1992–94.

There is probably some huge historical lesson to ponder in this dramatic cycle-of-life story as it has played out over the last 2,800 years. One that comes to mind is positive and reassuring: as cruel as history can sometimes be, this particular story has a

Peter Hatlie with students at the Roman Forum. *Anthony Mazur.*

relatively happy ending. Considering all of the options available, there is arguably no better caretaker for the memory of Bovillae and the physical preservation of the small part of it in UD's possession than a serious and excellent institute of higher learning like the University of Dallas in light of its deep commitments to sounding out, caring for, and reflecting on the ancient past. UD Rome will not be sponsoring an excavation anytime soon in ancient Bovillae, nor (despite the temptation) will its faculty and students be renting metal detectors and digging treasure trenches in order to unearth whatever may remain of the city in our own backyard. As long as the university maintains its presence on these hallowed grounds located above ancient Bovillae, however, it will continue to honor the debt it and all of the modern world owe to the cities, people, and civilizations that have shaped our modern identity to such a great degree.

INTERMEZZO. DUE SANTI WINES FROM THEN TO NOW

Michael Housewright

When I first arrived at Due Santi in 1992 as a matriculating junior going late to Rome, I found the place to be a rustic example of a rapidly changing Italian rural life. The property seemed to be heading toward dilapidation, and the old vines were trained high and spaced far apart for ease of working. The basic white wine produced there was rather innocuous, but the homemade grappa provided by the caretaker, Vincenzo, was potent and did the trick after a delicious lunch with him and his wife.

I was part of a cadre of strapping young men who had volunteered to assist Randy Irlbeck in moving some furniture from a nearby storage facility to the campus. At least that is how I remember it. But mostly I remembered Vincenzo and his wife and the fantastic lunch she whipped up in a matter of minutes. Randy sat across from me, and he could sense that I was enjoying myself immensely. His tutelage at the order of the Italian meal stayed with me and greatly influenced my life decisions for the next twenty-eight years.

In 1995, I had the rare opportunity to spend time on the Rome campus again while at UD. This time, I was a visitor during a semester studying in New York City. And as a visitor, I got to enjoy deeper interaction with the faculty and staff. I was twenty-four and unsure of what I wanted to be as an adult, but this Italy thing had clearly come over me three years prior and it would not let go. I got to know Dr. Wayne Ambler a bit, and on a little walk toward the dorm, he said to me, "We are going to make an ex-pat out of you one day." In 1999, I was a finalist for an administrative position

OPPOSITE, TOP
Due Santi Rosato and Rosso. *Vasile Chiriac.*

OPPOSITE, BOTTOM
The Due Santi Vineyards Team: Claudia Agrifani, Fabio Cinalli, and Peter Hatlie. *Michael Housewright.*

on campus but lost out in the end. However, I was not dissuaded from an eventual return to Italy, and by then, I had been working in fine wine for more than three years in Dallas. I knew I wanted to do something in Italy, and I wanted it to be with wine.

As I went on to grow in the wine profession and eventually cofound a travel company in Italy, Dr. Ambler and UD made the prescient decision to replant the white vines at Due Santi with Cabernet Sauvignon and Merlot grapes. In 2010, I tasted my first bottle of Due Santi Rosso 2009. In one taste, my dream of being involved in wine production in Italy and giving back to UD was born. I went the following year, where I met Dr. Peter Hatlie. I wanted to convince him that the wine could be a viable commercial product and could return a handsome profit to the Rome Program with some refinement and with someone spearheading the program in the United States. It took him a little time to trust me, but we have since become great friends and allies in the production and sale of Due Santi Wines. I enjoy using the plural because we currently make our delicious Rosso and a beautiful Rosato wine, with several other new products on the horizon.

And that is where I would like to focus. When I talked to Peter the first time, I told him that what I wanted to do was return the ancient cantina on campus to its former glory and, within ten years, produce the best wines in Lazio (our region where Due Santi and Rome are located). And we have taken several key steps to bring this to fruition. Our first was giving our exceptional winemaker, Claudia Agrifani, the directive to go for the top-quality wine she can manage from our grapes, which are certified organic and are another primary reason we have the potential for greatness in winemaking. We then took the step to hire one of the leading agronomy

PREVIOUS
The vineyard just before the vendemmia. *Michael Housewright.*

OPPOSITE, TOP
"O for a beaker full of the warm South" (Keats, "Ode to a Nightingale"). *Stephen Henderson.*

OPPOSITE, BOTTOM
"All the Shrines and Homes of men are consecrate with Vines" (Belloc, "Heroic Poem in Praise of Wine"). *Stephen Henderson.*

companies in Italy. Under their leadership in the field, we have planted a new vineyard dedicated to Cabernet Franc production (arguably the grape most suited to our soil and climate). That vineyard should produce its first crop in 2024. We are also replanting a portion of our Merlot vines that were most suited to simple wine with a much heartier clone of Cabernet Sauvignon. This plan, over the next three years, will finally allow us to produce a decadent reserve-level wine that we believe will be in the running for the best wine made in Lazio. That would be no small feat in the company of great producers like Fiorano and Colle Picchioni.

What we have created and are continuing to foster is the only single-vineyard organic wine produced by an American institution of higher learning. This is something of which we can be proud and by which we may profit. Every retailer and restaurant that sells our wine is directly advertising our university. When we begin to submit our wines for critical review, the pros will know the gravity of this project, and they will promulgate our unique story in many forms of media. I would attest that this project has the chance to be the route by which many new families learn of the university, and new donors intrigued first by the wine and then made enthusiastic about our academics will perhaps make generous gifts.

What does all of this have to do with higher education? We can look to scholarly history from Plato to Jesus Christ and even to our founding fathers to know that wine has been present and lubricating the contemplative mind for millennia. I would argue that when correctly applied, a beautiful Italian wine can assuage the angst of this modern era and can serve to bring collective intellect to the dinner table where the problems of the past and future can be appropriately assessed and duly solved.

CHAPTER 2

THE VILLA GABRIELLA AND THE HISTORY OF MODERN ITALY

GREGORY ROPER

Gustavo Piga parks a modest Fiat under the umbrella pines at Due Santi and climbs out. I've been deputized to greet him before his lecture to the students on the financial crisis of 2008 and its aftermath. What do you say to a professor of economics from the University of Rome? What do you say to a man as he comes back to a place he knew as his grandparents' home? Honestly, I'm a little intimidated. He was probably a young man, not much older than these Rome students, when UD came and swept this place away from his family, away from him, and I hear he hasn't been back more than once or twice since. I'm anxious not to say something that might dredge up unhappy memories.

"Hello," I say. "Welcome—welcome *back*—to Due Santi." It's all I can stumble out.

He looks up at the umbrella pines, around to the vineyard, and up toward the villa. "I am *so* happy the university took over this place, and kept it *so* beautiful," he says. He's a man about my age, balding like me, with a warm smile. His shoes, his tweed jacket and knit tie, aren't smashingly stylish in that intimidating Italian way. Suddenly he's just another academic, and he claps me on the shoulder and shakes my hand. "I'm Gustavo. We have some time before the talk, don't we? Can we go up to the villa?"

We enter the villa, and I unlock the doors to the *salone*. It's been kept as a lovely living room, a place where faculty parties are held, where faculty children celebrate birthdays—a fireplace, couches, a beautiful dining room table in front of the windows overlooking the tennis court. Gustavo takes two steps in and stops, taking in everything. He takes a deep breath and grins. "I can hear my grandfather right now. He would sit up here and blast Beethoven on his huge stereo with all the windows open." He gestures around the room, showing how it filled up with musical *Sturm und Drang*.

OPPOSITE
The Villa Gabriella.
University of Dallas Archives.

ABOVE
The Villa Salone.
Stephen Henderson.

"My cousin and I would be down below, playing tennis, and he would come to the window and tell us to keep it down; we were disturbing his music!"

We walk to the window and look down at that tennis court. He shows me where the glass broke when the Allied bombers dropped errant ordnance on what is now the field outside the *mensa*. "He never fixed that window. He always showed it to people and proudly said it was American bombers that did that. He was very pro-American, my grandfather."

This is the story of a family. It's the story of an unusual couple who came out to the hills beyond Rome, who built a villa and who were then almost immediately forced out of their home during World War II. It's the story of the family who returned after that war, raised three children, built friendships, weathered all the usual ups and downs of family life, forged an international set of relationships, brought grandchildren into this family, and saw the matriarch and then the patriarch die. Frankly, as Gustavo told me, "The story of the villa is the story of Italy in the twentieth century." It was a family of some privilege, true, but as the mother and then the father died and they had to make the difficult kinds of choices all families then make, they, with grace and generosity, allowed an American university to take over their beloved home so that thousands of young students could enjoy what they treasured. And it's a family who to this day love that we, the family of UD, are now a part of their family's history.

"My father was a *formidable* man," says Guglielmo, the eldest brother, Gustavo's *zio*, as we sit at the *forno* on a summer day, drinking wine and reminiscing. "He was Sardinian, and as we all know, the Sardi are known for their stubbornness. Oh, he could roar!"

"I could be terrified of him; I would hide under the table when he yelled like that," Gabriella, the youngest, the only daughter, says. "But he was quite gentle with me...."

"You were the girl!" Guglielmo interjects. "He yelled a lot but then was affectionate."

"But I know at first it was very hard on my mother," Gabriella continues. "She was very lonely at first—she told me—living out here all by herself."

For that time, they were an unusual couple: an unlikely international pair from opposite sides of the globe. Lorenzo Piga was born eleven days before the beginning of the twentieth century in a small Sardinian town, the son of the local lawyer and the daughter of a fine family. The Piga family owned more than half of the land in the village but lost it, Guglielmo noted, because his great uncle was "a scoundrel." Lorenzo made his way to the capital city, like many young men, to find a better life. In 1927, he found work with AGIP, the Italian oil company, and rapidly moved through the ranks. Edythe Kollerstrom was the even more adventurous one, the attractive twenty-five-year-old Australian school teacher who came to Italy to study the Montessori method—and, it seems, to get away from a failed romance with an Indian diplomat. When she left on the trip, she had no idea that she would not return home for many years. But she met Renzo, they fell in love, and in short order they married, on April 20, 1932.

"His hobby was horticulture," Guglielmo told me, to explain the move they made to the countryside in the late 1930s. "The company was offering the standard apartment in Rome to its young executives, but my father asked instead to take a sum of money, and from that he came out here and built the villa." It was an unusual move at the time; Romans tended to want to live in the city, near the life of urban culture and convenience. The Castelli Romani, and the corner of it down the hill from Castel Gandolfo known as Due Santi, were at that time much more remote, much more rural, than they are today. Renzo wanted to try raising sheep, growing fruit trees and

TOP Architect's original drawing of the villa. *Piga family.*

BOTTOM Guglielmo, Dario, and Gabriella Piga on the steps of the villa. *Piga family.*

grapes, and testing his hand at making wine. For Edythe, he later installed one of the first kiwi groves in all of Italy; Due Santi Romers from 1994 until 2008 will remember this grove next to the villa and the luscious fruit it produced. I once read a book on Italian cuisine that talked about the kiwi being brought to Italy and how today Italians love them so much they will swear they are native to the country.

The villa was completed in 1940, just as Italy was joining the war and Gabriella was joining the family; Edythe was not so excited about having another child, but both she and Renzo were ecstatic to welcome a girl, so they named the house Villa Gabriella in her honor. (Few UD Romers know the villa has a name.) "We were of course jealous," said Dario, "so our parents named the two umbrella pines at the front gate Guglielmo and Dario to placate us." (Even fewer today know that these two grand trees, at the old gate behind the villa, also have names.)

One gets the sense, talking to Dario and Gabriella, that Edythe didn't have much say in the decision to move to the *campagna*. "She was alone out here much of the time, as my father went to the city for work each day." The war years were particularly hard. For a time, it seemed that England had lost the war. Edythe and the children had to stop speaking English; if Renzo was away, she slept with a pistol under her pillow.

The Allied bombing started in 1943. Everyone knew the Castelli's high ground and railroad connections were significant targets, and Kesselring, the Wehrmacht commander, made nearby Frascati his headquarters for defending against the Allied troops slogging their way up the Boot. Accuracy, however, was not a strong suit in the bombing technology of the day, so often the family—and neighboring friends, farmers, and workers—would wait out these raids in the villa's underground cantina, which today still exists under the *forno* patio, where the wine casks are still stored. "We all had to be quiet and stop arguing," Gabriella said. More than once bombs landed on what is now the *mensa* field. "One time a young man went out too early, saying the bombing was all over, but it wasn't…he was killed," Gabriella remembered. "It was horrible."

After the Anzio landing in 1943, the Castelli became even more a focus of the war. UD students may know about the Nettunense, the road that splits off at the stoplights in Frattocchie and runs down to Nettuno, next to Anzio. This is the road that the Allies eventually fought their way up on their way to Rome; Aprilia, halfway down the road, where Renzo had a fruit orchard, was the scene of some of the fiercest, deadliest fighting. One fateful day, the Wehrmacht knocked on the door and gave the family forty-eight hours to get out. These two days were filled with furious activity—packing and hiding belongings; a false wall was constructed to hide valuables. (The faculty copier, on the bottom floor of the villa, now sits in the niche that was walled up.) The family moved to an apartment in Rome on the Via Savoia, not far from the Borghese Gardens.

Seven-year-old Guglielmo was a Balilla (the Fascist Boy Scout–like organization) and remembered the day when Mussolini was arrested. "I started crying and was surprised to see my father deliriously happy. He was the most internationally minded person in the office and was certain we would lose the war; 99 percent of Italians thought the war was won when France was invaded. Italians loved to divide up the spoils. Mussolini was not stupid, but he had never been outside of Italy; he didn't know the power of the Americans, of the British." Then came June 4, 1944, and the liberation of Rome. "The best day of my life," Guglielmo said; he tasted white bread for the first time, given to him by American soldiers. The Americans took over the villa in the spring of 1945, and when the family finally returned, Villa Gabriella was "a mess." The walls were black with writing and graffiti.

But after the war and the cleanup, the family grew into prosperity. Renzo flew to the United States in 1947 to negotiate with American officials about Marshall Plan funding, and when the family visited Edythe's brother in England in 1949, Renzo put a ceiling over the patio, extending the *salone*. Every Sunday became a kind of open house at Due Santi, with Renzo loving to grill and carve meats as he hosted cookouts. An international group including a Norwegian consul and his English wife; a lung doctor and his wife, Yvonne; and another couple, began to gather regularly; the four couples dubbed themselves the "Otto Santi" and enjoyed playing cards. Gabriella remembered the Englishwoman, Bunny, saying, "Let's go have a jolly cup of tea." Soon the pool, and later the tennis courts, were added as a way for the children to have something to do on these long summer afternoons. With ten acres in which to play, there was not always full supervision. The boys loved to find unfired ammunition from the war, empty out the gunpowder, and set it alight; one such explosion knocked down a small stone wall. Gabriella, excluded from the boys' play and always wanting to be a teacher, would set up her dolls and hold school, instructing them in all the usual academic subjects.

Meanwhile, the children were growing up. The local schools, Gabriella said, were "wretched," so they attended school in Rome—the boys at a *liceo* run by the Christian Brothers and Gabriella at a school run by strict nuns. "I broke my leg, and Dario had to carry me into the school. The nuns did not like that—boys were not allowed inside the school!" Frustrated at Dario's poor showing in school, Renzo made him a deal: if he could become first in his class, he would receive a Vespa, the new mode of transport transforming Italy (and featured so prominently in *Roman Holiday*). "In no time at all," Guglielmo said of his brother, "he was first in his class." Both of the boys met their wives through Gabriella, who was a magnet for many young men.

During this postwar time, a beautiful young woman, Adele, arrived to cook and tend the house for the family. "All of Dario's and my friends were in love with her and took their best chance" to date her, "but we were shocked" when she spurned all of them for Vincenzo Romano, a simple, sweet young man who had also arrived to tend to the vines, the buildings, and the grounds. Vincenzo and Adele stayed on the property for most of the rest of their lives; when UD acquired the land, they found a house a short distance down Via dei Ceraseti and continued to work on the property. They were the *nonno* and *nonna* of many a student, faculty member, and faculty child; one of the great events of my own life was harvesting olives with Vincenzo and my two sons in 2008.

In so many ways, as Gustavo had said at that first lecture, the history of Due Santi is the history of Italy in the twentieth century. The lead-up to the war, the war itself, the recovery, the Vespa—it's almost as if a Hollywood screenwriter, or a historian of the century, wrote the plot. Guglielmo's first car was a Cinquecento, that symbol of Italy moving again after the war. The children after school and university joined a kind of Italian diaspora in the prosperous 1960s. In a fascinating prelude to the connection with UD, Guglielmo worked in Texas—in Midland, for Phillips Petroleum, finding it "very cosmopolitan" as employees from around the world gathered in West Texas. "The Americans couldn't say Guglielmo," he laughed. Gabriella visited Guglielmo in Texas and then, while in New York, married a New Yorker, Don Carlos Dunaway, in 1963. His work in the film industry brought them to Los Angeles, but they soon moved back to Rome. Meanwhile, Dario's business was growing, and Renzo was trading successfully with the Saudis and the Kuwaitis. Soon grandchildren were coming to Due Santi on the weekends, sleeping in upstairs rooms.

That history continued in the 1970s, when Italy descended into the *anni di piombo*, the "years of lead," a time of economic shocks—particularly provoked by the oil shocks from Middle East wars and turmoil—and domestic terrorism. It can be strange for UD Romers, so full of the joy of going to beautiful Italy, to realize that the university started the program in some of the most troubling years in the country's history. Strikes and threats of violence were frequent; you can hear tales of these from 1970s Romers, who laugh them off, but there was real trouble in the country. Aldo Moro, the prime minister, was kidnapped and assassinated by the Red Brigades, his body left in the trunk of a car just off Piazza Venezia in the center of Rome, in 1978. (Imagine an American president kidnapped and assassinated, his body dropped a few blocks from the Capitol, or in Times Square, to consider how shocking this event was in Italy.) A bomb ripped through the Bologna train station in August 1980, killing eighty-five and wounding two hundred. In December 1981, just one month before my own Rome semester began, Brigadier General James Dozier, serving in Verona with NATO, was kidnapped from his own apartment by the Red Brigades.

Nicole Dunaway, Gabriella's daughter, remembered being prohibited from leaving the gate at Due Santi at this point, as it was deemed too dangerous and kidnappings were frequent. "We lived through that without really knowing," she said, as she was young at the time and Due Santi was a refuge. "We would come every weekend and most of the summer holidays," she said. "We lived endless summers there. We were free the whole day, but there was a strict schedule: lunch at 1:00, and then watching the *telegiornale* [evening news] every evening *a punto* at 8:00." She remembered an employee, Domenico, and his pristine white jacket with gold buttons, serving the family dinner. The economic shocks forced changes in the family as well. Renzo asked

Guglielmo to join him in the business, and Guglielmo started making contact with Soviet oil interests. He thought his father, so pro-American, might be upset, but he was not. "He was very pragmatic," he said. But the biggest blow came in May 1976, when Edythe died after a rapid illness. Gabriella had come home to be with her in February and stayed on to help her father before moving to the house in the Flaminio district, on Piccola Londra, where she lived with her second husband. Renzo slowed down, and the villa was slipping a bit. He considered moving to a nursing home, but Guglielmo talked him out of it. "I told him he'd be bored out of his skull and die in three years. Here he had family that loved him." So Renzo stayed on for another nine years. His own final illness took him on November 1, 1985, just a little short of his eighty-sixth birthday.

All of the family talks about their devastation at the death of the *paterfamilias*, not because he was loved more than Edythe, said Nicole, but because he was the center of the life at Due Santi. And immediately the family had to decide what to do with the villa. Would Guglielmo buy out his siblings? Would they cut it into apartments and sell or rent them? Nicole and Gustavo, then twenty and twenty-three, even had the idea of buying it themselves, but none of the family could quite make these plans work and they reluctantly sought a buyer for the property. Gabriella talked about it in terms of "sorrow" and "desolation" but also said that "it was too hard to keep the lovely, too-big old place with none of us living there."

And again the history of modern Italy parallels the story of the villa, for who stepped in to purchase their beloved home but an American institution—not a wealthy financier or a Hollywood movie star, but a strange little Catholic university that had recently lost its lease on the home of its superb Rome Program and was looking for a permanent home. But that transition is a story for the next chapter.

It's a beautiful, mild summer evening in 2017, and the Piga family have assembled back at Due Santi for the first time in many years. Nicole has asked Dean Peter Hatlie for permission to celebrate her fiftieth birthday on the campus, and all day long friends and the extended family have arrived. A chef from a favorite restaurant has been brought in to prepare a meal for dozens. The party moves from the pool to the *forno* patio and eventually to tents and tables set up on the *mensa* field. And what is simply wonderful is the gratitude every member of the family offers to me, to Dr. Hatlie, and to the university for having preserved their family home so beautifully and kept it a living home. I ask Nicole what struck her most when she returned. She pauses, considers for a moment, and says, "The smell. I always remember the smell of Due Santi." Her mother, Gabriella, and her cousin Gustavo break into big smiles and agree. When I ask if the day has been bittersweet, Gabriella immediately

THIS VILLA
WAS FOR MANY YEARS
THE CHERISHED FAMILY HOME
OF
RENZO PIGA
AND
EDYTHE KOLLERSTROM

OPPOSITE, TOP
Renzo and Edythe Piga with their granddaughter Nicole. *Piga family.*

OPPOSITE, BOTTOM
Plaque above the front door of the villa. *Vasile Chiriac.*

says no. "You know, it was always a very international place, Due Santi; an Italian and an Australian. I married an American, as did Gustavo; there were the Otto Santi from other countries as well. We are all so, so happy that that the university came here and that it remains such a beautiful, international place."

I wish Nicole a happy birthday and slip away at a respectable American time so these Italians can continue the party late into the evening. As I say goodnight, she tells me, "When I dream at night of home, I dream of Due Santi."

INTERMEZZO. *GLI ITALIANI*

ANDREW MORAN

Romers over the last decade feel not only gratitude to Nino and Nuccia for the delicious meals that they and the *mensa* staff serve daily but also affection for the campus's jovial *nonno* and generous *nonna*. Students returning to Irving in the last two years also speak with particular warmth about the Chiriac family, who have quickly made themselves indispensable. But great thanks should be extended, too, to people whose names the students may not know—Mabel Bianconi, Iza Pichalski, and Giovanni Hanu—whose work keeps the interiors and exterior of campus beautiful.

TOP Silvia De Simone. *Rome Campus Archives.*

BOTTOM Vincenzo and Adele Romano. *Rome Campus Archives.*

OPPOSITE Nino Tripodi. *Stephen Henderson.*

In fact, the professors and student life assistants quickly learn of their utter dependence on the Italians and recognize that while they may have their two years in the sun before heading back to the United States, it is the permanent staff who keep Due Santi running and make it such a happy place to work and study. For more than a decade, the Americans have relied on Silvia De Simone in the Business Office and later her assistants Alessandra Morello and Benedetta Barbieri to acquire needed documents, keep the books, and arrange trips—in fact, to get most anything done. For more than two decades, they have marveled at how Fabio Cinalli, now assisted by Tiziano Cavalletti, can both run a vineyard and fix *anything* he puts his hands to. That tradition of excellence goes back to the caretakers of Due Santi who

stayed on after UD bought the property. For half a century, Vincenzo and Adele Romano looked after every building and nurtured every flower and fruit tree before, as the campus's original *nonno* and *nonna*, they did the same for many a student and faculty family for a decade. It is for that more important tradition, of friendship and hospitality, that the university owes even greater gratitude to its Italian hosts.

INTERMEZZO. FAMILY LIFE: A "COR" CURRICULUM

Lisa Mobus

If the core curriculum is the heart of the University of Dallas, then the Rome Program is the heart of the core, its animating energy and distillation. Those who have experienced Rome as students have found family there; those who have also lived there as families are doubly blessed.

My father, Dr. James Fougerousse, had a hand in the program's founding, so Rome was part of my consciousness from earliest days. As a teenager on campus, I acquired new "aunts" and "uncles" (we were not so formal as to address my parents' friends and colleagues by titles, nor so informal as to use just first names) and many older siblings. Some of those students I still number among my dearest friends, members of my chosen "family." In the spring of '82, even though I was only fourteen, John Norris and his friends took me trekking around the Eternal City, which made me feel very "grown up." John is dear to me to this day—the big brother I never had, the godfather of one of my children, a true and generous friend that I never would have gained without living on the Rome Campus.

ABOVE Lisa and Jeff Mobus. *Rome Campus Archives.*

OPPOSITE, TOP Proud fathers Steve Bird and Peter Hatlie with Abigail and Iola. *Rome Campus Archives.*

OPPOSITE, BOTTOM The prosecco flowed freely at Caroline Reedy's birthday party. *Ivanna Bond.*

I saw my UD education through new eyes when I returned in the fall of 1987 for my own Rome semester. My father was the director, and I realized that my experience in Rome connected the threads of my childhood to my nascent adulthood. Young Sybil Novinski was my roommate, as she had been freshman year. We had taken ballet lessons together in Irving as little girls and played while our fathers talked or worked on a sailboat the Novinskis co-owned with other UD families. At fifteen, we went together with our fathers on the Greece trip. And yet, returning to Greece with Sybil and our fathers, traveling throughout Europe with classmates and reading core texts, especially Augustine's *Confessions*, I finally understood that the core curriculum teaches one to examine profoundly one's judgments and one's heart. It awakens one to the *wholeness* of truth, justice, and love. It is the role of a family to instruct its children in such pursuits, which the Rome Program did for me.

My final UD Rome experience involved building my own family. My husband, Jeff, and I moved to Rome in 1991 with four suitcases and returned to the United States in 2000 with four children. In the intervening years, we enjoyed a new "family," with professors and their children, such as the Amblers, Criders, and Franks. Birthdays were celebrated at the round table near the *forno*. In the villa *salone*, there were the children's performances, such as the adaptation of Shakespeare arranged by a young Catherine Ambler. Although now scattered throughout the United States, we follow one another's moves and our children's milestones from afar, especially through new technologies that permit this continued familial closeness.

Jeff and I finally returned to Roma last summer, to celebrate our thirtieth wedding anniversary, and our hearts were home. Without these experiences of family at UD Rome, our lives would be much poorer.

CHAPTER 3

A UD *AENEID*

The Founding of Due Santi

Andrew Moran and Gregory Roper

"*Tantae mōlis erat Rōmānam condere gentem*" ("How great a task it was to found the Roman nation"), sang Virgil in the proem of *The Aeneid*. And how great a task it was to found the permanent Rome campus. Like the Trojans, the University of Dallas had lost its home, Hotel La Villa on Via del Pescaccio—not burned to the ground by vengeful Greeks (although considering its condition by 1989, that would not have been a bad idea), but our lease not renewed. Again like the Trojans, UD then had its years of wandering, five as opposed to the Teucrians' seven, not on the Mediterranean and in Crete, Carthage, and Sicily, but on temporary campuses in Vitinia and Manziana. Like the Trojans once more, a sense of *pietas* provided strength to overcome ceaseless adversity, our household gods the great classics of the West, our revered ancestors Socrates and Sophocles, Peter and Paul. The UD story differs, however, in that it does not revolve around a single hero. We have an Aeneas, but in this epic father Anchises plays a more significant role than he had in *The Aeneid*. There is not only an Ascanius but also Aeneas's second son, Silvius. Quite appropriately for a university that recognizes the necessity of tradition (from the Latin for "handing over"), a number of individual talents handed over to successors the great tasks of preserving the Rome Program and founding the new campus. Indeed, in the university's Roman epic, as the burden became greater each step of the way, an older man passed on to a younger man some new great task so that it is a story with four protagonists: the President, the Visionary, the Unsung Hero, and the Builder. The heroes—if not swift-footed and lovely haired, at least great-hearted, much-enduring, resourceful, and laughter-loving—found and built in the Eternal City a permanent home more beautiful and suitable to the flourishing of UD students than anyone could have imagined.

THE PRESIDENT

Robert Sasseen, a political philosopher from the University of Chicago by way of San Jose State, became president of the University of Dallas in 1981, at a moment of crisis after some tumultuous years. Sasseen, who died in 2017 at the age of eighty-five, was not charismatic and would never become a legendary figure, as were Donald and Louise Cowan, but he brought stability and began his fourteen-year presidency overseeing the construction of the Haggerty Science Building and the Church of the Incarnation. But no task was greater than the purchase and construction of the Eugene Constantin Rome Campus, popularly known as Due Santi. It was only in 1988 that he learned of this new burden. The university had moved into the Hotel La Villa, located off the Grande Raccordo Anulare on the way to Fiumicino Airport, in 1973, and while its condition declined over the years, it still served its purpose: a site with a classroom, a cafeteria, and beds (and one hour of heat per day in winter) two bus rides away from St. Peter's Basilica. Francesco Stoppini, its owner as well as UD's longtime Roman patron, had brought UD there early in the Rome Program's history. He remained a generous supporter, even after his death in 2018, through a Rome scholarship established in his will. But he sold the property in 1986 to his daughter Dina, who had different plans for it. In 1987, the university learned that it could no longer use the hotel in the front of the property, including its *mensa*, so students were crowded into the three "towers" in the back and the lounge was turned into a substitute *mensa*. In May 1988, the university learned that its lease would not be renewed.

Should UD close shop and leave Rome? Some thought so. But Bob Sasseen had Provost John Paynter lead an academic review of the program, which came to the same conclusion as that of nine thousand Romers over half a century: "The Rome program is central to the education provided in the Constantin College of Liberal Arts." The study also noted something practical, that "the Rome program is essential to undergraduate recruitment and retention." But it was an outside consultant, Spruell & Company, that recognized something not quantifiable but more essential, that missed trains in Munich and Felliniesque follies in Florence were as important as Lit. Trad. III: "UD must demonstrate that there is something to fulfill a sense of adventure. The Rome Program offers that opportunity." And so, like hopeful Anchises

Brian Whalen and Robert Sasseen (wearing red ties) with Erik Norberg-Schulz (*third from left*) and members of the board of trustees at the *forno* patio. *Rome Campus Archives.*

in burning Troy, Sasseen became convinced that a new home awaited and recommended to the board of trustees that the Rome Program continue at a new location.

But the president now faced a very Roman question, *Quo vadis*? ("Where are you going?"), as well as a universal one, "How are you going to pay for it?" His attempt in 1981 to launch a capital campaign had fizzled, and a new lease elsewhere seemed the likely solution for a university without cash in hand. But Sasseen saw that purchasing a property would better serve the university's long-term financial interests, and of course, a home of our own would better serve our educational purposes. He told board members, "We're going to do this; I can get the money"—and he ultimately did. Stoppini initially suggested that UD buy the Via del Pescaccio property from his daughter, but the first hero of the story had a grander ambition. To fulfill it, he turned to its second, a scout, like Caleb sent by Moses to espy the land of milk and honey (to switch heroic narratives), the first to see the fated new home.

THE VISIONARY

What's a UD tale without Jim Fougerousse in it? Who else but the hero of *The Groundhogiad* could first make landfall at Due Santi? In the 1984 mock epic, dispossessed beer-swilling adolescents seek, Telemachus-like, their missing father figure Foug to save Groundhog from the administrative equivalent of the evil suitors. But in 1988, Dr. James Fougerousse (class of '67), rather than another Odysseus, was another Aeneas. A bear of a man with broad shoulders and chest and a booming voice to match, he had always been a visionary for UD. In 1963, he had been one of the freshmen who started Groundhog. His time in Europe the following year led him to see the university's need for a common undergraduate experience like his own. He had left for Germany after his sophomore year and, after learning the language, had ridden a motorcycle through Communist Yugoslavia to Greece. Upon his return a year later, he strode into President Donald Cowan's office in Carpenter Hall and said, "We need a program in Europe." Cowan, a physicist, having just attended a desalinization conference in Greece with his wife, Louise, the architect of the core curriculum, agreed. In 1969, Cowan sent the recent graduate to Rome to negotiate with Sister Georgianne Segner, Mother General of the School Sisters of Notre Dame, for the university's use of the order's empty Generalate House. And so the Rome Program began in the fall of 1970. By 1981, Fougerousse was teaching English and German at Via del Pescaccio and soon was appointed campus director.

The university's lease prevented a man of vision from ordering matters as he might have preferred. But Fougerousse's little skirmishes with the management paid off in small victories. The eventual purchase of washing machines freed the students from dependence on a laundry service. The authority to purchase and distribute toilet paper won plaudits from nineteen-year-olds accustomed to American largesse.

The great victory would come only after what seemed like a great defeat: the loss of Via del Pescaccio. President Sasseen sent Fougerousse to find a new property, and with Dr. Brian Whalen, the assistant director, he drove around Rome in the fall of 1988, looking at vacant religious houses and other buildings in Parioli, in Mussolini's modernist EUR, and in Vitinia. But they were quickly drawn to the Castelli Romani south of the city, especially to the area around Marino, which stood out for its location and beauty. They considered the Helio Cabala Hotel in Marino and a sports complex in Santa Maria delle Mole before Stoppini, through Bishop Dante Bernini of Albano, learned about a family, the Pigas, looking to sell a villa off the Via Appia, between Marino, Albano, and Castel Gandolfo.

Like smiling Aeneas on first seeing the Tiber telling his steersman "turn the prow to land," Fougerousse on first seeing Due Santi recognized it as the site of the new campus. On their first visit, he and Whalen snuck around the property and took photos through the bushes. From the top of the driveway, he quickly had a vision of how Due Santi could become the University of Dallas Rome Campus. "He had such an imagination," said Whalen, "that he could see the possibilities." The two did exhaustive research on the Villa Gabriella and the location, including on public transportation, but alas, their report to Sasseen that the Cotral bus to the metro stop at Anagnina was a "fifteen-minute" ride would soon be rendered inaccurate by the effect of suburban sprawl on traffic. But the more important reasons they gave for why UD should purchase the property were that it was an analogue to the Irving campus—set apart but not too distant from the city and so ideal for academic and student life—and it was beautiful. This vision of Due Santi remains true.

After thirty-five years with the University of Dallas, Jim Fougerousse would soon leave for the German-speaking lands that he loved, first off to Liechtenstein and then to Gaming, Austria, where he founded Franciscan University at Steubenville's successful program. But his influence at UD continued, especially through two young men he brought to Rome, the protagonists in the second half of UD's *Aeneid*.

THE UNSUNG HERO

"I owe a lot to Jim," said Brian Whalen. "He took a chance if he liked you." The university would then owe a lot to Whalen, Fougerousse's appointed successor, an Ascanius to his Aeneas. He is not so well remembered at UD today as the other protagonists since his time with the university was not so long. But in a critical period of two and a half years, he shouldered the load. Whalen had been a doctoral student at UD and then with his wife, AnnMarie, served as a resident assistant in Irving. Her thesis on Giotto's Scrovegni Chapel (maybe the greatest masterpiece in Italy that Romers typically miss) brought them in the summer of 1986 to Padua and then to Via del Pescaccio, where they met Fougerousse and his wife, Sally. Fougerousse, a good judge of character, hired them for Rome the following year. Whalen would succeed him as campus director at the age of twenty-nine, the same year he became a father and defended his dissertation, at a time when that position meant not only the usual duties of running the program and keeping rambunctious students in line but also engaging in delicate negotiations. In this most complicated part of the epic, the purchase of Due Santi, Whalen was, however, one unsung hero among many. From the spring of 1989 to the spring of 1991, he teamed up with a number of other men of patience, intelligence, and good will, both Americans and Italians, to fight off a host of bureaucratic monsters and secure UD's ownership of Due Santi.

In the spring of 1989, UD entered into an agreement to buy the property and put $200,000 down to show its intentions and secure the process. But the sale hit a snag as the land had to be re-zoned, and so UD was introduced to the complex world of Italian politics. Giulio Santarelli, the Socialist Party mayor of Marino, was in favor of the sale, seeing it as good public relations to have an American university in his *commune*. The *regione* of Lazio opposed it, however, and put roadblocks in its way. And even with Santarelli's support, Marino wanted more out of the deal, at one point even asking for a public swimming pool. Although Wayne Ambler and his family, because of the earnest money, were allowed to move into a Villa Gabriella that had fallen into disrepair, for a year the deal sat in limbo.

But Whalen was not without Italian friends. Carlo Spani, who understood the Anglophone world well, having an English law degree, acted as a bridge between two cultures. Fougerousse had long used him as the university's Italian lawyer, and during this time, according to Whalen, he "gave us good tactical advice." Dario Piga, the second son of Renzo, was similarly helpful as the university sought to buy his family's property. "He was an honest, good person," Whalen said. "He told us about the intrigue, about how to get things done within the system."

Meanwhile, back in Texas, a fundraising campaign with a target of $3 million ($6.3 million in 2020 dollars) ramped up and continued for several years. The strength of the dollar against the lira at that time made the project attainable. The board's plan was to borrow half of the total and raise the other half. Trustees Jim Moroney, Brian Smith, Robert Power, Ed Haggar, Eugene Vilfordi, and Paul Lockhart were all important in this effort, working with Vice-President of Finance Jim Bellinghausen. The Constantin Foundation donated $400,000 and promised up to $1 million in a matching grant. While an alumni phonathon raised only a disappointing $76,000, the parishioners of the Chapel of the Incarnation pledged $98,000 for a campus chapel. Later, in 1998, the Lieutenant Eric Hamm Gate was added through the gift of $14,000 from the Hamm and Papania families.

But in 1990, there was as yet no guarantee that present and future generosity would bear fruit. Eventually, Whalen, Piga, and Spani sought to break the impasse in the most appropriate way: with a great meal. A large delegation from Irving—President

Sasseen; new vice-president of finance George Herbst; trustees Vilfoldi, Haggar, Smith, Moroney, and Lockhart along with their spouses; the mayor of Irving, Bob Prince; and five other officials and their wives—all gathered with Marino and Lazio officials at the Hotel Helio Cabala for a full-on blow-out dinner where wine was poured and friendships were made. The TV show *Dallas* was all the rage in Italy, and this helped grease the social wheels. And in the Italian way, these personal introductions and friendships grew into negotiations by which the roadblocks were put aside. Both Whalen and Randy Irlbeck are adamant that "UD never offered or paid any bribes or did anything illegal." Instead, rather than a swimming pool for the community, the university agreed to build a water treatment plant—past the end of the vineyard and soccer field, below the dorm—that would serve not just the new dormitory and faculty apartments but also the questionably constructed houses across the Via Appia that had inadequate connections to Marino's water treatment plant. The zoning was approved, ruffled feathers were smoothed, and the deal was on.

The closing papers were signed on October 1, 1990—eighteen months after the first agreement. The cost was ₤1.7 billion, or $1,367,692. What the university acquired was a 10,000-square-foot villa, a cantina with apartments above it (soon to become the *mensa* and faculty apartments) of some 10,000 square feet (with an additional 2,500-square-foot terrace), more than an acre of gardens, and ten acres of farmland. All of this would require extensive renovation to turn it into the functioning UD Rome campus.

In the spring of 1989, Whalen had brought the last Via del Pescaccio students to see what the university hoped would be its new home, and the following semester, he and the students presented the architectural plans for the campus to Pope John Paul II at the papal summer palace in Castel Gandolfo. Now in 1990, the Fall Romers were brought from the temporary campus in Vitinia to Due Santi to celebrate what was no longer a hope but a promise. Needed now was a second son of Aeneas, another young man, one who had learned some arts from his grandmother Venus's cuckolded husband, the bandy-leggéd smith, the Lord of Fire, Vulcan.

THE BUILDER

To identify Randy Irlbeck, from the unincorporated Texas Panhandle farming hamlet of Kerrick (population thirty or so), with Silvius, Aeneas's Roman-born second son by his Italian wife, Lavinia, may be a stretch. His two eldest children were born in Italy, not he. Nonetheless, he arrived at a young age and spent enough time working for UD

Rome, in one fashion or another for almost fourteen years, that when he spoke Italian, people from other parts of the Boot thought him Roman. Just as Silvius succeeded his half-brother Ascanius as king of Alba Longa (the modern Castel Gandolfo, just up the hill from the new campus), so also Irlbeck eventually succeeded Whalen as director (with Father Gilbert Hardy, Pat Daly, and John Norris manning that position in between them).

Jim Fougerousse had brought Irlbeck to Italy in 1986, after he graduated from UD with a BA in physics, to be the Rome assistant, back when there was only one. After three years, in 1989, his work for UD seemingly was done. He returned to Dallas, waited tables at TGIFriday's, worked the early shift for UPS, and had interviewed to join EDS, Ross Perot's software firm, as a trainee, a difficult position to acquire. But that fall, Denise Schuler, the director of the Irving Rome Office, had a difficult pregnancy, and Irlbeck was asked to step in and run orientation for the Spring Rome class. When Schuler went into early labor, Irlbeck took over even more duties, all without pay, until Mary Laughlin, the HR director, said to him, "I think you're working for us; we can actually pay you"—in this very UD way, Irlbeck became an employee again. In October 1990, after volunteer work in the Dominican Republic and while living with the Novinskis, he was asked to return to Italy as Rome Campus construction coordinator. He politely turned down the prestigious position with EDS, hopped on a plane to Italy, and moved into the villa. When renovations began there, he moved to an unheated apartment in Grottaferrata. He was twenty-six years old. In a year, he had gone from waiting tables at Friday's to being in charge of a $3.5 million construction project in a foreign country. "We were just young pups," Irlbeck said about his and Whalen's role in the founding of Due Santi. But his appointment was an inspired choice. Irlbeck's input was crucial, for as a former student and assistant, he knew the daily life of the students and professors; he knew how the Rome Program *worked* and could ensure that the developing campus would serve UD's unique needs.

The architects had already been chosen. The American ambassador to Italy had suggested the firm of Bill Ahrens, which designed hotels across Italy and the Mideast. Lyle Novinski recommended Erik Norberg-Schulz, son of the famous architectural historian and theorist Christian Norberg-Schulz, and the work was split: Norberg-Schulz would create the design, and Ahrens's employee Vincenzo Vannini would take the plans from there. Norberg-Schulz and his partner Adriano Mariani were, in Whalen's words, "young, creative, idealistic," and "they came up with a great design." The dormitory would be a medieval fortress on the outside, a Renaissance palazzo on the inside; the third floor would resemble a monastic cloister. A diagonal rotation of the building would bring light into the lounge, while defining the piazza and terrace.

Randy Irlbeck and Bob Galecke, vice-president for finance, with a student. *Rome Campus Archives*.

Forty rooms would serve 120 students, with a maximum of 142 if they become quadruples (a design never pursued). There were to be no stereos or TVs in the dorm lounge. The Aula Magna would be in basilican form, with a capacity of 160. Thus, the design reflects the very nature of the Rome Program itself, teaching and leading through the use of forms and spaces.

But while there existed an ideal form, the unruly matter needed much shaping. The site of the dormitory was still vineyard. What would be transformed into the *mensa* was a cantina, storing a dozen wooden one-thousand-liter casks and the Pigas' other wine equipment, now long idle. On the

site for the Aula Magna was a large, two-story metal barn that would have to be completely removed. A shed by the vineyard stored old farm equipment. Conditions on the third floor of the villa, where Irlbeck slept, remained primitive, as water was still supplied through the cistern. On the second floor, the library and bathroom had yet to be converted into a chapel; the downstairs had become a depository for fifteen years' worth of odds and ends from Via del Pescaccio.

In the spring of 1992, all appeared ready for the hammering into shape of the new campus. At a groundbreaking, the beloved Cistercian Father Hardy blessed the site and laid the first stone. The construction firm Boccadella, from the Abruzzi, went to work. Almost immediately, however, authorities from Marino stopped work for a supposed "abusive construction," even though UD had obtained the proper permits. Construction was delayed until the summer.

As in any construction project, there were problems to confront. "The cantina really should have been torn down," Irlbeck believes; all-new construction could have provided for more space. But the decision was made to work with the existing structure to provide a sense of the historical space. More troubling was the concrete slab supporting that metal barn structure, as it was not strong enough to hold the Aula Magna when filled to capacity. The footprint was widened and new support walls added several feet out; fortuitously; these created space for the RC offices and the storage behind the cappuccino bar. But this major new project in 1993 threatened to delay the completion date of the entire construction. In the same way, the beams under the chapel, judged inadequate to hold the weight of the altar and a full congregation, had to be taken out and re-structured. All the while, the dollar was falling against the lira, creating an administrative and financial nightmare that made it difficult to track real expenditures and costs. Irlbeck designed a Lotus 1-2-3 program to track prices, purchases of lira, and spending, largely solving the difficulty.

OPPOSITE, TOP
A crane over campus during construction of the Aula Magna. *University of Dallas Archives.*

OPPOSITE, BOTTOM
The dormitory nearing completion. *University of Dallas Archives.*

By mid-1993, with the dormitory beginning to take shape, Irlbeck had to consider the furnishings and design of the individual rooms. He spent significant time at Euromobilia, a furniture store, and in the electrician's shop. Laughing, he explained how he chose bunk beds similar in design and construction to those used in Italian prisons: "I knew those would take years of use, and when married couples came to visit, we could take them apart and put two together to form a *matrimoniale*." The plumber on the project was helpful as he had lived in New York, spoke some English, and understood what Americans wanted. Likewise, Irlbeck, with his experience of campus life, understood what students in the morning rush needed: he wanted the bathroom to allow five of the six suitemates to occupy it simultaneously, so students could get up, get moving, and be on time for class. Thus, he asked for two sinks, two showers, and a separate space for the toilet, something the Italians on the project had not considered. The furniture—the desks, the beds, the "totem" containing a night light and a book niche for each occupant and topped by a light to illuminate the whole room—all were custom designed for UD students' use. Ceiling fans were rare in Italy, and none had lights, so the rooms had to get light in other ways. "We spent a lot of time and attention on these things," he said. The tile, other flooring, all of the finishes, were chosen with an eye to the needs of the students and the program.

"We're going to make it." In early 1994, there was a general optimism that the Due Santi campus would be ready for the fall semester. But the dedication, planned for June 11, was another matter, and the scramble to have campus ready for it was intense. At the beginning of June, there was still no functioning laundry room, and even the furnishings in the dorm rooms, where trustees were to stay, were incomplete. Spring Romers from the Manziana campus stayed on to help, but still, as the date approached, the director of advancement wanted to call off the celebration. But the builder led faculty,

OPPOSITE, TOP
Francesco Stoppini and Marilyn Walker at the opening celebration. *Rome Campus.*

OPPOSITE, BOTTOM
Plaque by the *forno* honoring Randy Irlbeck. *Vasile Chiriac.*

This Campus
Was Constructed In Great Part
Thanks To The Hard Work,
Dedication, And Care
Of
Randy-Lee Irlbeck

staff, and students through one last spasm of furious effort. Irlbeck recounted that "Glen Thurow [the provost] was sitting on the floor in the villa *salone* re-wiring a chandelier three days before the dedication." In the end, it was "one of the most fun weeks of my life," said Wayne Ambler, who came back from Irving for "a mini-UD Rome" of lectures, site visits, and dinners with the assembled group. The Cowans and Novinskis attended, as did dignitaries such as Bishop Emeritus Tschoepe, future bishop Gregory Kelly of Dallas, and Pio Cardinal Laghi. "The campus was far more beautiful than I imagined possible," said Ambler, noting that the landscaping and the inaugural events were both "terrific" and that "the Advancement people did a great job." Mass, blessings, and, in true Italian fashion, dinner completed the culminating day. For Irlbeck, though, there were still two months to go. He bought American-style washing machines, oversaw renovations to the pool (reducing it to four feet throughout for safety and putting in a new liner and decking), completed flooring and furnishings, and renovated the *forno* area.

The new semester in August began with Mass at St. Peter's and a walking tour of Rome, which, as always, were followed by the Greece trip and Ten-Day. One Rome semester continued to follow another, such that twenty- and seventy-year-old former Romers share a common experience. But August 1994 was nonetheless different. The wanderings of the Trojans—from the School Sisters of Notre Dame Casa Generalis to the Scalabrini Brothers International Center; a long sojourn at our Carthage, the Hotel La Villa, Via del Pescaccio; the Villa Santa Cecilia, Vitinia; and the Hotel degli Etruschi in Manziana, near Lago Bracciano—were over. Through the efforts of the four protagonists highlighted here, and scores of others in Texas and Italy, the great task was completed. While the founding was not of Virgil's ideal city of laws that would reshape the destiny of the world, it was of a campus where students encouraged to pursue truth, wisdom, and virtue through study could flourish in preparation for their own destinies.

INTERMEZZO. THE ROME CAMPUS EXPANSION

ANDREW MORAN

In 2016, in response to the growth of the university and the wear and tear of twenty-two years, Dr. Peter Hatlie, director of the Rome Program, instituted the Rome Expansion and Renewal Campaign. Friends of the university responded generously, and so today's visitors to campus will find it even better suited to the needs of students and more beautiful than ever. The expansion of the *mensa* and the addition of an annex to the dormitory allow for approximately a dozen more students per semester. There is as well a new soccer field at the end of the vineyard and a new exercise room. A new pedestrian entrance near the Via Appia keeps students from having to walk down the narrow and increasingly busy Via dei Ceraseti. Instead, they go past an addition to the vineyard to a new pavilion that offers maybe the most beautiful view of the campus and, from there, walk down the rose path of the vineyard.

PREVIOUS
A side view of the new dormitory annex. *Stephen Henderson*.

TOP
Ribbon cutting for La Casa di Zach Annex. *From left to right*: Peter Hatlie, Barry and Kathy Clark, and John Plotts. *Stephen Henderson*.

BOTTOM
A game on the new soccer pitch. *Vasile Chiriac*.

OPPOSITE
A view from the new pavilion. *Stephen Henderson*.

CHAPTER 4

SEEING DUE SANTI

The Sense of Place

Daniel Milligan

Here is the Capitol where in the old days a human head was found, and this was declared to be an omen, for in that place would be fixed the head and supreme sovereign power of the world.

–*Livy*

The plan of a building is a human appropriation of space. We walk about the plan; our eyes look forward, for perception is sequential; it takes place in time; it is a series of visual events, just as a symphony is a series of auditory events. Time, duration, sequence, and continuity are the constituent elements of architecture….Architecture, through the plan and section, is closely akin to music.

–*Le Corbusier*

To describe the University of Dallas's Due Santi campus as idyllic is not an exaggeration. This may seem paradoxical given its location relative to the bustling city just a few miles away, but clearly the combination of the landscape and the architecture has a profound effect on how we view and experience this special place. How is this possible? The answer lies at the root of why we travel to this place to begin with, as well as how certain places profoundly shape what we feel and how we think. That a building or natural environment can affect what we feel implies that some places have a connection beyond reason. That a building or natural environment can do so reveals that places have an ability to draw people to them not only because of what may have happened there but also because what happened there is manifestly dependent on that place. Rome is such a place, and Due Santi is ideally positioned to reveal the truths and paradoxes of Rome to those who search for them.

In his influential work *Genius Loci: Towards a Phenomenology of Architecture*, the architectural historian and theorist Christian Norberg-Schulz attributed to the surrounding environments of Rome the unique characteristics that we find reflected in the city itself. One such characteristic, found in the landscape north and west of the city, is the soft brown tufa connected to pre-Roman Etruria. The tufa houses natural carved out passageways, what Norberg-Schulz called "a kind of 'urban' network of paths." Vernacular stone structures in medieval Roman streets are formed seemingly not by addition but subtraction, as many streets give the impression not of being the space between buildings but rather of being carved out of the earth, of being the space created when the earth is excavated and cleared away, much like in an Etruscan necropolis.

This chthonic quality is opposed, almost diametrically, by the Alban Hills. This realm is not under the earth but takes dominion over it. There is no mystery as to why upstart gods chose this landscape as their home. This land was truly fit for the gods and their architecture. The two volcanic lakes in deep craters, Lago Albano and Lago di Nemi, help to reinforce this idea of the elemental relationship between mass and space. It should come as no surprise that the main sanctuaries of Latium were located in the Alban hills. The gods were at home there. The temple to Jupiter Latiaris sat atop Monte Cavo, while on the slopes leading down the crater to the mystical calm of Lago di Nemi was the home of Diana on one side of the lake and of Juno on the other. Monte Cavo was thus the absolute center of the region of Latium. The importance of these sites and their alignments was not lost on the Romans, and these organizing principles united the entire region. Thus, what happens in Rome is manifestly dependent on the uniqueness of that place.

The idea of imposing order on the landscape through this expansive axis is even more impressively observed within Rome itself. This imposed order inextricably links the urban center of Rome with the countryside and with the Alban Hills in particular. Roman town and military planning—though ironically not Rome itself, which is not based on a grid—is most essentially marked by the existence of the *cardo*, the main north–south axis of the settlement, and the *decumanus*, the dominant east–west axis. In the legend of Romulus, what is architecturally significant in his settlement of the Palatine Hill is the Roma Quadrata. The name implies four quadrants and perhaps even a *cardo* and a *decumanus*. What is more, the Via Sacra, or the main road that united the conurbation of settlements that surrounded the hills in ancient Rome, formed a distinct and undeniable *axis urbis*, an implied but definite

Entering Due Santi.
Vasile Chiriac.

organizational and unifying line through the settlements and, later, the city. It was this axis that knit the early settlements together; most profoundly, if this axis were extended in both directions, it passed through in one direction the Temple of Jupiter on the Capitoline Hill (where, as Livy tells us, an intact human head was found) and in the other direction directly through the Alban Hills to the south of the city. The urban center is thus linked to the old center in Latium and the seat of the gods.

The lessons of Roman planning and architecture inform the design of Due Santi, and the skillful implementation of these lessons allows us to feel not like a mere observer of life or a visitor in the Alban Hills while on the campus but rather like a resident, a citizen who shares in this Roman experience. Anyone who approaches the *Colli Albani* from the direction of the city and travels down the modern Via Appia may have much the same experience Cicero did on his journey to his villa in Tusculum. The immediate scenery is disregarded, and we are drawn to the beacon that is the

The Business Office and dorm. *Vasile Chiriac.*

Alban Hills, the home of the Roman gods. We are traveling the *axis urbis*, on that connection between the gods in Latium and the center of Rome. This is the environment that we experience upon arrival at Due Santi, and there is no opportunity to deny the connection between the city of men and the realm of the gods because we occupy the crossroads, our own *cardo* and *decumanus*. Upon entering the Due Santi campus gates for the first time, we find our eyes moving along with our feet. We traverse the long driveway, under the row of umbrella pines and past the pool and bucolic villa, while glancing out over the slight undulation of the vineyards. We approach the office, pass the *mensa* under the shade of the loggia and approach the heart of the campus, the Tyrrhenian Sea shimmering in the distance. Students, professors, maybe an alumnus sipping wine in the summer—all are reclining at sunset in the piazza, taking in the views. The space itself offers an invitation to join them and brings strangers together.

Due Santi as we experience it, as we walk down the driveway, reveals itself as a Roman urban form, with a distinct front and back. By the very nature of the landscape itself, the campus also reveals itself as a distinct enclosure. The topography assists in this impression. The lush and manicured campus grounds and vineyards give way to larger, more uncontrolled growths of vegetation at the perimeter of the campus property. This subtle delineation of landscape gives a powerful sense of enclosure while allowing a continued link with the surrounding landscape. It establishes a distinct inside-outside relationship. Thus we are reminded of the campus as enclosure while also being able to view outside and beyond it. The campus would be experienced quite differently, and to its detriment, if this natural boundary did not exist. The sense of inside-outside on the campus would be greatly compromised, and its sense of enclosure would be greatly diminished. The piazza is often described as the urban room. Successful public spaces employ a common architectural language along all of their boundary surfaces to create this sense of enclosure. Openings in the urban room are small enough that our mind completes the enclosure and disregards the opening, thus creating the architectonic whole. This happens at Due Santi via the landscape and topography, perhaps accidentally, but it may be one of the most powerful ways that the place may be experienced as a cohesive unit.

Rome, of course, delights the traveler with its renowned buildings, but to understand its hold on us, we must recognize our emotional response to its carefully considered spaces. Here we must move away from considering the region-wide connections and axes established by the ancient Romans and look at the fabric of the city itself. This requires experience on a smaller, intimate scale, and Baroque Rome certainly was skillful in influencing our emotional experience in certain spaces. The sixteenth-century plan of Pope Sixtus V (1585–90) connects major monuments and spaces in the city by a series of broad, straight avenues. The obelisks that reside in the piazzas or in front of monuments are visible down Sixtus's compact plan of straight streets. The city is thus respectful of pedestrian scale, while the urban room of the piazza serves to knit the city together. A street sweeper or tourist in Piazza Navona has an experience that rivals that had by Pope Innocent X in the 1650s upon visiting his family's Palazzo Pamphilj. In this spirit we should then consider the experience of Due Santi.

In the early twentieth century, Le Corbusier advanced the idea of experiencing architecture via the architectural promenade. We would encounter a series of framed views at carefully considered locations through a continuous circulation path, a series of visual events over time. Le Corbusier applied this to the interior spaces of a building, but this same idea organizes the campus at Due Santi. Its interior spaces are functional, but we still deeply appreciate the campus, just as we do the experience of Rome, as an urban room, but now transported to the Alban Hills. The original villa begins the core of the campus and is closest to the gates on the axial path through the campus. Not surprisingly, the residential structure is home to the most intimate spaces on campus. The diminutive but serene chapel and elegant *salone* are the two important public spaces in the villa. Standing in the high-ceilinged *salone* on the *piano nobile* and looking out toward the rest of the campus descending the gentle slope below, we appreciate the pleasing proportions of the space and, on looking down, the remarkable and rustic terrazzo floors, which call to mind *pietra dura* or the grand Cosmati designs found in Rome's more cosmopolitan spaces.

The space outside the villa, the patio and *forno*, forms a cool shelter under the pines. This is the place to retire to in the heat of the summer, closed and shaded, the opposite of the exterior space at the other end of campus, the open, light, and expansive piazza that adjoins the dormitory building. The campus is organized so that both of the major domestic buildings are provided with exterior spaces. These exterior spaces have distinctly different characters. The villa has this more intimate exterior room and even recalls the primal spaces of Etruria with its carved out rooms and small wine cellar below the *forno*. The campus may also be thought of as a series of spaces that start closed and progress toward open. The villa and *forno* provide this sense of being closed, of intimacy and privacy, a sense of being in and of the earth rather than above it, which gradually gives way to the revealing of the grand open spaces at the more bustling, light, public, opposite end of campus.

Perhaps of equal importance, the campus is organized in such a way that the very heart of the place, the piazza in front of the dorm, is farthest from its gates. Imagine the difference in its feeling if we entered the gates and the majority of people had no reason to traverse the length of the campus to reach their rooms. Instead, the location of the buildings fosters interaction and community. Now consider the framed views. The views are not framed by walls and ceilings or the elements of buildings, but by nature; they are integrated on the walk through the campus so that we experience the views as part of the architecture. The architect had the humility and skill to scale and locate the buildings properly and then simply get out of the way. Sitting in the piazza and looking beyond campus—be it toward the Tyrrhenian Sea, the vineyard, or graceful Castel Gandolfo—it is impossible to think "what the campus really needs are more enclosed man-made circulation spaces."

The small piazza in front of the dormitory is a dynamic space skillfully composed. The large block of the building has undergone a rotation in the landscape; after a straight path from the gate to the piazza, the dorm angles away from us. Absent this rotation, the small piazza would be too contained by building surface—the space would lose its considerable view and be stripped of its vitality. The slight rotation directs one's view to the countryside below. It breaks that axial relationship,

"A rotation in the landscape." *Vasile Chiriac.*

but it breaks it for a very good reason. The dynamic view is enhanced by the breaking of the static orthogonal relationships and extends our experience of the space into the landscape beyond. The directed view leads the eye to the horizon in all directions, and as we bring our eye back to the small piazza, we are reminded of the sense of enclosure the campus provides.

It is also in this space that we find the amphitheater, the campus's only instance of the manipulation of section—that is, of creating exterior space by excavation. The sectional change of the amphitheater reinforces the importance of the space while joining the student lounge with the exterior. It further energizes the space to have this sectional change, the amphitheater, accessible to pedestrians while joining and

FOLLOWING
"The manipulation of section." *Vasile Chiriac.*

expanding the social heart of the campus in the piazza with the cappuccino bar. The Aula Magna classroom—basilican with its nave, implied apse, side aisles, and clerestory windows—announces its importance as a space and joins the intellectual center of the campus to the social one found just outside. This campus core unites the vitality of pedestrian space with the sublime beauty of nature in a manner that sparks a visceral emotional response. It is this response that is at the very core of experiencing buildings as architecture. It is this response that makes simply being at Due Santi such a pleasure.

The dormitory building anchors the piazza. Its slightly splayed walls seem to grab the landscape, as if to ease our fears that rotating the building off the prevailing axis was accidental and that further slippage may be imminent. Its mass reassures us that this is exactly where it should be. Its plan also reassures us. The plan recalls both Roman *insulae*, the apartment buildings of the working class, and the *cortile*, or the central open courtyards of Renaissance and Baroque palaces. This is a fitting metaphor for the domestic heart of the campus. The interior courtyard seems almost an extension of the exterior piazza, as the voiding of the rotated corner at the entrance of the building provides a transition that manages to feel both interior and exterior. Once inside, there is a feeling of being in a distinct and independent space as we reorient ourselves along its axis, much as Romans walking through the Forum did thousands of years previous.

Even after traversing the path many times, there is still a desire to make the journey again, to experience the process of revealing that begins at the gates and ends at the small piazza in front of the dormitory. In the piazza, we may contemplate the nature of the sunlight and its effect on the character of the buildings. It is in the warm Roman sunlight that this character is best revealed. At these times, the walls seem almost to pulsate with the warmth of the sun, and their massiveness seems soft, as the pastel pink, orange, and terra-cotta colors work to dematerialize the buildings, not by opening them up structurally like a Gothic cathedral but by emphasizing that primal chthonic quality—that they are of the earth itself. This allows the buildings to give the impression of almost being fused to the site, appearing as if they were always there, as if the earth was simply cleared away to reveal them. They are truly of that place. This permanence also calls to mind the medieval fortress, a building form that still exists seemingly because of its sheer mass. It is of that place, and it cannot be moved.

It is this emotional response that we experience at Due Santi that gives the place meaning. That response reveals that the Alban Hills are part of what makes the city of Rome unique and contributes to the aesthetic pleasure that the campus provides. The forms of antiquity and the Baroque that we experience in the city are the generative ideas that govern the campus planning. We experience the grandeur of Rome and

return to the bucolic setting of Due Santi, and those experiences are subtly echoed all around us. We are eminently fortunate to be the guardians of the spirit of this place, and in exchange for this guardianship, this place reveals itself to us. This is the joy of experiencing Due Santi.

PREVIOUS, TOP
Teatro Due Santi, aka the amphitheater. *Vasile Chiriac.*

PREVIOUS, BOTTOM
A Renaissance cortile. *Vasile Chiriac.*

ABOVE
Due Santi at night. *Vasile Chiriac.*

INTERMEZZO. CHRISTIAN NORBERG-SCHULZ AND THE UNIVERSITY OF DALLAS

Gregory Roper

When I was in graduate school at UVa, putting day-old bagels on the table by teaching a composition class and tending bar, one of my part-time jobs was being the office manager for a small architecture firm in Charlottesville. Once I had the job, I was asked why I was interested in architecture, so I told them about my Rome semester: my introduction to Classical, Medieval, Renaissance, and Baroque buildings; my learning to look at them and experience them; and how it changed the way I saw things. "We were taught by this funky little Norwegian man who was just great. His name was, um, Norberg-Schulz."

The place went silent.

And then, all five of the firm's architects were crowding around my desk. "You had *who* teaching you?" "Christian Norberg-Schulz? Really? What was he like?" "How did he lecture? What did he teach you?" "How on *earth* did you get to study under Norberg-Schulz?"

And that was the day I discovered how lucky I had been—or yet another way I had been so lucky—to be on the UD Rome Program in the 1980s, as well as how foolishly I had virtually wasted the experience. For that sweet little Norwegian man, whose Italian wife taught me Survival Italian (and whose daughter is a renowned opera singer), was nothing less than *the* most important thinker at many architecture schools around the country, UVa one of them, as well as simply one of the top theorists of architecture in the entire world. His *Existence, Space, and Architecture*; *The Concept of Dwelling*; and, especially, *Genius Loci: Towards a Phenomenology of Architecture*, shaped generations of late twentieth-century thinkers and practitioners. *Genius Loci* has been called the most important book on architecture in the twentieth century. Norberg-Schulz developed through Heidegger a new way of conceiving architecture as the phenomenological experience of space, as the way a particular spirit (genius) presides over a space. In 1978, Lyle Novinski convinced the Drs. Cowan to invite him to UD as the McDermott Lecturer, and as was the case in those days, he spent a week on the Irving campus, lecturing and meeting with faculty and students. He enjoyed UD so much that when he returned to his home in Rome, the relationship continued, and he would lecture a few weeks

Christian Norberg-Schulz leading a tour. *Rome Campus Archives*.

each semester to us sleep-deprived, just-back-from-a-long-weekend Romers or take us around the city to teach us S. Maria in Trastevere or S. Andrea and the Baroque.

When it came time to design the Due Santi campus, UD called on Christian's son, Erik, who transformed the Piga villa and outbuildings into a beautiful space for learning—a phenomenological experience, as Danny Milligan has shown, in line with his father's vision and UD's notion of education. In this way, Norberg-Schulz the younger gave UD the gift of his father's vision.

And we just thought of him as the sweet Norwegian man who pronounced *Renaissance* funny and who would get so excited showing us the slide of Bernini's staircase that he would attempt to climb up into the slide to demonstrate how it shaped our experience of the space. No one bothered to tell us whom we had at the front of the classroom. Maybe it was better that way.

But my friends at the firm never got over their envy.

INTERMEZZO. THE CHAPEL OF THE TRANSFIGURATION

Lyle Novinski

Having been involved since the Rome Program's beginning, leading students to Greece, teaching art history, and giving summer tours for adults, I quickly agreed when Provost Jack Paynter in 1989 asked me to design the chapel for the newly acquired campus. I had stayed at the villa and knew the space he suggested. We then enlarged that space to include not only the master bedroom but also the bathroom, closet, and hall, incorporating another window and allowing more seating.

There was a need for a chapel to center the spiritual life of the students and resonate with the aesthetic experience of the program. But it required a significant name, a theme. At Due Santi one evening shortly thereafter, the beauty of the place inspired a name fundamental to the Faith: Transfiguration. It both emphasizes the transformative experience and reminds the students that they must go down from the mountain.

A fundraising evening at the Cruises' and the generosity of the Chapel of the Incarnation's parishioners raised the $100,000 needed to create the Chapel of the Transfiguration. I made a scale drawing of the altar area, including the Transfiguration mosaic. Father (now Bishop) Greg Kelly, then chaplain in Irving, accompanied me on my next trip to Due Santi. We taped the drawing on the end wall of the bedroom, the altar end—it fit perfectly.

The design intentionally relates to the students' Rome semester. The altar shares the dimensions of the altar placed by Saint Francis at San Damiano in Assisi, reflecting the old harmony of numbers in the medieval world. Its column has eight sides, relating to the Incarnation form. The Transfiguration mosaic recalls Raphael's great painting in the Vatican Pinacoteca. The windows are onyx, like the window at the altar apse in St. Peter's and those in the church in Orvieto. I'm told that at the fall equinox, the spots cast by the blue and green rondels—symbols of heaven and earth—align themselves down the center aisle and fall on the altar at the halfway point in the season.

My daughter Sybil, a Rome assistant, inspired by the floor in Raphael's Chigi Chapel in Santa Maria del Popolo, selected the oval pattern on which sits the altar. The Renaissance reserved the circle, with its single focal point, for images of perfection—thus its use in the design of our tabernacle. The oval, containing multiple foci, reflects the inclusion of the People of God.

TOP
The Chapel of the Transfiguration. *Vasile Chiriac.*

BOTTOM
Icon of the Due Santi, Peter and Paul, donated by Lyle and Sybil Novinski. *Vasile Chiriac.*

Mosaic of the Transfiguration executed by Julie Richey, from a painting by Lyle Novinski. *Vasile Chiriac.*

Following the tradition of seeking a unifying theme for sacred architecture, care was taken to integrate simple forms into a cohesive composition. The rosewood chairs also gather history, being the *mensa* seating from the old campus. Their scale fit the space perfectly. Dr. Bill Frank's sons sanded and oiled the bases, and Randy Irlbeck found a craftsman to replace the pink vinyl seats with cross-shaped rush.

The lectern and candlesticks are of a similar wood, padouk, and repeat the square dimension of the chair legs. Constructed in Irving by myself and my sons, they were carried in my luggage and assembled for the dedication. The perfect column of the tabernacle awaits a golden metal surround suitable for adoration. I found the Stations at a shop near the Vatican. Sybil and I were pleased to gift them and the Due Santi icon.

But the chapel still awaited its major work, the Transfiguration mosaic. Alumna Julie Richey, an accomplished mosaicist, copied my full-scale painting, and I raised the funds, about $95,000 including a donation by Trustee Peggy Thompson honoring the late President Donald Cowan. After two years of meticulous labor, the mosaic was shipped and installed. It is a pleasure to know that the Chapel of Transfiguration supports the spiritual and academic life of Due Santi and provides a discernable resonance with life in the Eternal City.

CHAPTER 5

STUDYING FACES

The Rome Semester Curriculum and Travels

ANDREW MORAN

There is nothing new under the sun—so sayeth the Chronicler of the University of Dallas Rome Program. One generation passeth away and another generation cometh, but the curriculum and the group trips standeth forever. So it seemed at the faculty-staff dinner in Athens in the fall of 2015 after Ryan Reedy, the assistant dean of the Rome Campus, burst our balloon. Because of the next day's excursion, we had begun the meal with more than the usual excitement occasioned by the prospect of an evening of rooftop dining with the Plaka below us and *taramosalata*, *moussaka*, *saganaki*, and octopus on our plates, with *ouzo* and *mastiha* to follow. We the tan-faced children, we the youthful sinewy race, would be the first UD Greece trip to go down to the Piraeus to catch a boat to the islands of Ydra, Poros, and Aegina in the Saronic Gulf, to take up the task eternal of exploring temples, swimming in the wine-dark sea, and buying trinkets. Pioneers! O pioneers! But Ryan then shared with us three yellowing pages that Father John Bayer, O. Cist., had found in the papers of Father David Balás of happy memory, the Patristics scholar of international renown who in the mid-1970s taught in Rome. "ITINERARY ESPECIALLY PREPARED FOR GROUP UNIVERSITY OF DALLAS" informed us that on Monday, October 6, 1975, almost forty years to the date earlier, for the price of 600 drachmas, students could enjoy a day trip to three islands on a boat leaving from the port of Piraeus. Vanity of vanities, sayeth the Chronicler, and all is vanity.

But in fact, although the Greece trip assumed its general shape from the very beginning, it has undergone little changes from time to time, as have the trips in Italy.

Likewise, the curriculum has been tweaked, most notably in the 1980s by Dr. John Paynter. This chapter will look at the books and cities of the University of Dallas Rome Program, including changes in them both small and large, considering their purposes. A look back at what is past and what has changed not only is of nostalgic interest but also by contrast reveals what is essential about study in Rome, travel in Europe, and the relationship between the two for University of Dallas students. The semesters in Rome do beginneth and endeth and beginneth again, for five decades now the pattern largely the same—the same books, the same cities. But because of that pattern, there may be something new under the sun—at the semester's end something new in the students, involving their aspirations, their understanding of what Rome offers them, and even the way they see faces, including their own.

A Tub of Books on the Wine-Dark Sea

Until recently, Due Santi students began the semester by hauling up to their rooms a hard red plastic laundry tub, full to the brim with five courses' worth of books. In the last of the books they read, *The Tempest*, Prospero and his daughter, Miranda, miraculously arrive on a near-deserted island after being set adrift in "a rotten carcass of a butt," but the gentle old counselor Gonzalo, out of pity for the most bookish hero of the Western literary tradition, had filled the decrepit tub with volumes from the magician's library. To an English professor, at least, it was a delightful coincidence: like the hero "for the liberal arts / Without a parallel," students at the study-abroad program that can make the same boast began their adventures with a lot of books in their tubs. Not every (now metaphorical) tub over the years has been identical, for a variety of reasons. Departments have redefined their courses. For example, Philosophy, when renaming the Philosophy of Man course Human Person, required the Rome professor to end the semester with a work of his own choosing by a twentieth-century Catholic thinker (Max Scheler's *Ressentiment*, St. John Paul II's *Love and Responsibility*, and Josef Pieper's *In Tune with the World: A Theory of Festivity* were the first three). The presence of professors with particular expertise has allowed for the occasional elective to be offered, such as Dr. Wayne Ambler's Xenophon and Dr. Peter Hatlie's Byzantine Greek. Italian language students drop one of the regular offerings to continue their study, and Western Civilization II (in addition to Western Civilization I) was once regularly offered. So, too, were courses on mathematics and American politics taught when faculty from those departments came to Rome.

But in the early 1980s, John Paynter, the university's provost, decided that the same five courses would be offered every semester, and so they have been: Art and Architecture of Rome, Human Person (formerly Philosophy of Man), Literary Tradition III, Western Civilization I, and Western Theological Tradition. Various one-credit courses have popped up, such as People and Places of Rome, as did a second philosophy course for students ahead or behind their classmates in the core sequence. But his decision to link together these five has stood the test of time, as not only is it practical—sophomores earn hours in core classes before they return to Irving to devote themselves to study in the major—but also the grouping works to impart a distinct intellectual character to UD students, one that often changes their direction in life.

Since the theology course, formerly not mandatory for non-Catholics, is now required of all students, and since Western Civilization II, once paired with the other history course, is no longer offered, five disciplines are studied in Rome, meaning five different ways of knowing. The world may be known through rational inquiry, through revelation and reflection on it, through poetry and performance, through historical study, and through images—the last of particular importance in such a text-heavy curriculum. Save for the scientific method and mathematical reasoning, the Rome semester courses provide all the chief means by which the world may be made intelligible. But this diversity in approach is accompanied by a unity in subject matter. That unity could be seen as a deficiency. As the second history course is no longer taught in Rome, the semester does little to treat the modern world, and indeed the core curriculum as a whole spends comparatively little time on it; the modern is treated at UD, but primarily through the majors. The different disciplines impart their own perspectives on it, as UD's little world mirrors the loss of a common perspective in modernity. While Philosophy does have the students read Nietzsche and a twentieth-century Catholic author, Theology has little time to explore the Second Vatican Council, and English no longer teaches any twentieth-century play, concluding instead with *The Tempest*. Lit. Trad. III ends with Miranda excited about the "brave new world," but she will only get to know it after the play ends, on leaving for Naples (the "New City," what its original name, Neapolis, means in Greek), just as our students will only study it in depth back in the new city of Dallas.

Instead, study in the Eternal City is chiefly concerned with old cities and old places. In one way or another, all the courses begin with Greece and move west, to Rome or to one of its daughter-cities. "Greece," of course, means a lot of things and a wide expanse of time. The Western Civilization course inevitably casts the widest net, from the age of migrations to Alexander and the loss of political independence. In Art and Architecture of Rome, students learn to distinguish between the Archaic, the Classical, and the Hellenistic. Lit. Trad. III has as its purview the Golden Age of Athens, the time of Aeschylus, Sophocles, and Euripides; since "the owl of Minerva flies at dusk"—the great ages of philosophy often coincide with the beginning of cultural decline—the philosophy course's Greek authors date from the following age, the fourth century BC. The discipline of theology obviously comes much later, in the Christian era, but that course, too, has a Greek base, those early Church Fathers who with their nimble Hellenic intelligences could make the kind of creedal distinctions then beyond the reach of Western Christians.

In privileging the Greek over the Roman mind, the core curriculum reflects the philhellenism that has characterized the West since the beginnings of Romanticism in the late eighteenth century, what the Germans call *Griechenthusiasmus*. "Do not teach him one word of Latin," W.B. Yeats wrote to his son's schoolmaster, encouraging instead study of Greek literature, "the Roman people were the classical decadence." Save for Virgil, there is not one word of the authors who had been the core of Dante's and Shakespeare's educations—Cicero, Horace, and Ovid—even in Rome. The students only read some of Livy's ironic yet heroic history of early Rome and maybe some of Plutarch's Roman lives. But it is not so much through these texts or the ancient monuments that students best encounter the direct and practical yet bold mind of pagan Rome. The deficiency in the core is more than made up for in the Art and Architecture course, from trips to museums such as the Capitoline, where in the busts students see those real Roman faces—lined, balding, individual, their intimate, frank gazes expressing not visions of Olympian perfection but the struggles and triumphs of this life. Still, it is in a book that Romers apprehend the richest expression of the Roman mind—that mind, still attentive to the things of this world, after it has encountered the Hebrew heart singing in the Psalms and the Divine Lover calling in the gospels. "Our hearts are restless until they rest in thee." *The Confessions* of St. Augustine, the last great author of ancient Rome and the first of the Christian West, is usually taught in two classes, both philosophy and theology, and in the semester's very middle, a preeminence that it merits. The initial thrill of Rome has worn off, and there is a growing sense that the semester is not only offering new pleasures and adventures but also demanding, in a soft but insistent voice, that one answer old questions: Who are you? How will you live your life? For students religious and not religious, *The Confessions* demands introspection and speaks to them as does the statue of Apollo in the Rilke poem: "You must change your life."

In Shakespeare's *Julius Caesar*, Cassius asks Brutus, "Can you see your own face?" In response to the answer no, he offers to be Brutus's "mirror." In the second half of the semester, that Augustinian quest to know one's true face continues, most especially in *Hamlet* and *King Lear*. "Who's there?" begins the former. "Who is it that can tell me who

I am?" screams the mad king in the latter. In the classroom, the focus has largely moved north, to Florence, Paris, and London, the great cities of an intellectually and artistically thriving Christendom, but these are daughter-cities of Rome, as are all the cities of the West, bequeathed by it that drive to consider particular faces as well as the Augustinian yearning to see ourselves in relation to our creation by the God of love. While it was back in Delphi that Apollo had enjoined pilgrims to "know thyself," it was in the West, more interested in history than in archetypes, that this work of addressing the question "What does it mean to be human?" yielded the richest array of answers.

Aquinas, Descartes, and Nietzsche provide students in Human Person varying images of man, but so, too, do the characters of Shakespeare. Hamlet holds the mirror up to the unweeded garden, to the spotted soul of his mother, to Claudius trembling in an agony of conscience, but the only image he sees reflected is the sinner bound for the putrefaction of the grave. Lear at first sees only his royal (and infantile) self, but he learns through suffering that we possess nothing but love and so dies brokenhearted holding the corpse of his daughter Cordelia, the very picture of love. *The Tempest*'s Miranda exclaims, "How beauteous mankind is," but her now worldly-wise father ends the play acknowledging how in need it is of mercy.

Even Western Theo. Trad. turns to different visions of humanity. The controversies of the early Church concerning the Trinity and the person of Christ were literally theological, having to with God, *theos*. But the Reformation was at heart an anthropological (from the Greek *anthropos*, "human") dispute, Luther and Calvin in one camp, the Catholic theologians at the Council of Trent in the other, all arguing about to what extent has sin marred human nature and whether then human works can cooperate with divine grace in the work of salvation. But even from Catholic Italy, in the different Davids of Donatello, Michelangelo, and Bernini, Rome students in Art and Architecture contemplate images reflective not only of the stylistic difference between the Early Renaissance, the High Renaissance, and the Baroque but also of three different conceptions of heroism. The value of the core curriculum is not that it is interdisciplinary, but that the disciplines come together, most powerfully in Rome, to compel students to recognize the various ways we may actualize the possibilities in our humanity before they choose their paths in life.

TRAVELS IN ITALY

Most semesters now offer a final group trip, three weeks or so before exams, to Venice and Florence (and Assisi if there had not been an earlier weekend trip there). Previously,

"And when she took unto herself a Mate, / She must espouse the everlasting Sea" (Wordsworth, "On the Extinction of the Venetian Republic"). *Michael Housewright.*

a quick optional trip to one of the cities served as a dress rehearsal for Greece, but this alteration has worked very well. Cash-strapped after Ten-Day and weary of being responsible for their own food, travel, and lodging, students appreciate six days and five nights of the program taking care of these, and the trip is a final opportunity for the class to travel together. That said, rather than the troop movements of the Greece trip—120 students, faculty, and staff marching from the Pnyx to the Areopagus or up the hill from the temple of the mother goddess to the theater in Delphi—on this trip professors and staff each take ten or so students on a walking tour one day and to some particular site the next. In Florence, a science major may visit the Museo Galileo, a history buff the Palazzo Vecchio, a sculpture enthusiast the Bargello and so on.

But the deeper wisdom in having a longer Northern Italy trip near the semester's end is that now the travel corresponds to the classroom. In the midst of their study of the achievements of Christendom, students travel to the places that reflect the genius of the High Middle Ages, the Renaissance, and the Baroque. And those three cities are so distinct that each exemplifies a different good to which one may devote oneself, again complementing the students' reading, again reminding them of the necessary questions: who are you and how should you live your life? Venice was the greatest trading city of its day, the first modern city, its merchant-adventurers the Warren Buffetts and Richard Bransons of the late Middle Ages and early modernity, and thus a sign of the great splendor and power that may come from the pursuit of wealth. That pursuit does not necessarily mean selfish luxury; Venice's wealth enabled its *scuole*, its confraternities, like the Knights of Columbus and the Shriners today, to pursue charitable works. Mercantile republics such as Venice (and the United States) have their virtues. Yet Venice puts off many students. While some are transported by the almost Oriental splendor and mystery, others are suspicious of its artificiality. The triumph of wealth and artifice, a city of palaces floating in a lagoon, from another perspective merely symbolizes greed and vanity, Venice's stage-set façades covering crumbling interiors sliding into the Adriatic as hypocrisy covers sin. Iago bewitches Othello through that double-image, tricking him into thinking that his seemingly (and in fact) virtuous wife, Desdemona, must be hiding something. Venetian women "let God see the pranks / They dare not show their husbands." And yet if one has the opportunity to return and walk around its less visited *sestiere*, one finds that the decadent image is the superficial one. There is another Venice, honest but dying, expressive of a noble history, composed of people whose lives are defined by their families and their neighbors, their work and their churches.

Florence also provides two images of life, and again Shakespeare captures this in *Othello*, a play read that semester in Lit. Trad. III. Like Claudio in *Much Ado about Nothing* and Lucentio in *The Taming of the Shrew*, Michael Cassio is a

polished Florentine who speaks beautifully and seems noble. Shakespeare apparently read Dante, as these Florentines, like their compatriots in *Inferno*, care only for their names. Cassio laments after the shame of getting drunk, starting a brawl and losing his position, "Reputation, reputation, reputation! O, I have lost my reputation! I have lost the immortal part of myself and what remains is bestial. My reputation, Iago, my reputation!" Modern Florence, too, provides the example of a noble exterior concealing a hollow core. Florence, designated a UNESCO World Heritage Site, hosts thousands of American students in study-abroad

Florence at sunrise.
Patrick Goodman.

FOLLOWING
Assisi, including the Basilica of St. Francis, from the Rocca Maggiore.
Stephen Henderson.

programs, which typically offer "cultural literacy" and some knowledge of history and art, which is good but is not the same as a liberal education that aims to turn souls to the love of truth and virtue. For too many students, a few minutes before *David* in the morning justifies five shots for five euros to begin the evening at one of the many British-style pubs that cater to American students. UD students are not immune to this appeal. Nonetheless, it is exhilarating to be in the cradle of Christian Humanism for students whose alma mater was born of its ideals. How can one not honor a city that for centuries, despite a population less than half that of Irving, would produce in every generation two, three, a half dozen geniuses—Giotto, Dante, Arnolfo da Cambio, Boccaccio, Donatello, Brunelleschi, Ghiberti, Botticelli, Machiavelli, Leonardo da Vinci, Michelangelo, and on and on? No other Western European city has ever possessed such a Greek sense of *arête*, and yet it is a Roman Catholic city, where the Franciscans served the poor at Santa Croce, where the Dominicans hosted theological disputations at Santa Maria Novella, and where Saint Philip Neri prepared to renew the Church of Rome in joy while honoring the memory of the severe reformer Savonarola. The dome of Brunelleschi, seemingly at one's fingertips from the Hotel Universo, UD's Florentine home for decades, symbolizes this paradox: it is the glory of the cathedral built for the glory of God *and* the glory of the city of men who know themselves without peer. It's hard to return to suburban mediocrity after walking those streets with a heart beating for the glory of God and His creatures. Florence stands for the life of the mind and of the hand, for culture in the sense of the best that has been thought and made, yet culture that has not been severed, as in the contemporary world, from cult.

The worship of divine glory takes on a humbler guise in the city of *Il Poverello*, "the little poor man." There is no confusion about what Assisi represents: the life of the spirit and the self-denial and charity it calls one to.[1] To regard this identity as meaning simply the mumbling of beads in dark chapels misses how the example of Saint Francis appeals to the whole person, including the body. No other group trip is so physically demanding as Assisi with its hills, especially if one eschews the modern road for Francis's path through the woods to the Hermitage. Most importantly, Assisi offers a new way of seeing ourselves. The last few years' spring Rome classes, in a hall in the convent next to the basilica that honors the saint, have

1. Assisi does have a second, less sacred aspect, as the marketplace of the world's tackiest religious goods. What I cannot imagine ever being surpassed are the figurines, for years on sale in a shop on the Piazza del Comune, commemorating the Circumcision of Christ, once celebrated as a universal feast day on January 1, as when Christ first shed His blood: the baby Jesus lay with His legs strenuously crossed, while the rabbi standing above held his knife as if he were Sweeney Todd.

listened to the five professors, sometimes joined by the chaplain, each give a ten-minute talk on what Saint Francis and the Franciscan movement have meant for his discipline. What emerges is that the intense Franciscan emphasis on the Incarnation and Christ's physical suffering, on God becoming one of us by taking on a body, led to not only the renewal of painting, poetry, and theater but also a revolution in the consciousness of Western man that was a precursor to Renaissance Humanism. Francis so loved Jesus that he became like Him. This Dante well represents in the *Paradiso* when Saint Thomas Aquinas of all people tells a tale of a knight-errant in love with a beautiful lady. Francis pursues and takes as his bride Lady Poverty, as had Christ, and the questing knight dies possessing the stigmata, again as had his Lord. In offering such a perfect reflection of Christ, even in his body, Francis points his mirror at a very different object than does miserable Hamlet or devious Cassius. Assisi is always a student favorite: its serenity is welcomed in the midst of a hectic semester, and some bold (or foolish) souls return bragging of having stormed a castle.[2] But every semester there are at least a few who realize that Assisi's greatest gift is Francis the painter and painted, he whose picture of Christ in himself—then pictured by Dante, Cimabue, and Giotto—is a model for all sorts of new pictures done in the style of the old masters.

TRAVELS IN GREECE

The Greece trip does not picture forth for students various ways of life as do the cities of northern Italy. After Delphi, no one aspires to imitate Apollo; while the Florence of the *Quattrocento* was the Athens of its day, the Athens of today does not, like today's Florence, still remind one at every turn of the life devoted to art and culture. So, what exactly is the academic purpose of the Greece trip? Does it make sophomores profess the Nicene Creed with more zeal and read Aristotle's *Metaphysics* with greater understanding? It's fair to say that for most students, Greece means ten days away from their books and is instead memorable for epic gyro-eating contests, nighttime swims in Nafplion's phosphorescent waters, and rambunctious ferry rides across the

2. It is best if students, in the attempt to avoid the Argus-eyed Rome assistants when sneaking out of their hotel to break into the Rocca Maggiore, do not walk on the roofs of the snoring citizens of Assisi, who, startled by the noise, may then, not without cause, confront them with pitchforks, as some Fall 2006 Romers learned.

Adriatic (or frightening ones if the winds are blowing the boat into mined Albanian waters during the Cold War).[3]

Then again, that joy in being young is an essential part of the Rome semester and is for students often most deeply felt in Greece. Bliss is it then to be young when the early October sun tans one's face on top of the Parthenon or when the year's first wildflowers in Olympia make coronets for previously demure young ladies. The stories brought back from Greece—of young men, after curfew, running the twenty-six miles from Marathon to the hotel in Athens; of a bonfire on a hilltop attracting the notice of Olympia's police; of hikers after dark lost on Mount Parnassus—are the stories of the glory and idiocy of youth. Greece's modern cities are not symbols of particular paths in life, but the places, themselves reminders of the young springtime of the West, inspire students to realize the glory and folly and joy that belong to youth.

The destinations of the Greece trip were established almost immediately. Louise and Donald Cowan had toured Greece in 1963 and visited Olympia, Nafplion, Epidaurus, Mycenae, Athens, and Delphi. Louise suggested these sites to Father Damian Fandal, OP, the first Rome academic director. For decades, Lyle Novinski, having flown in from Irving, moved counterclockwise toward Delphi, while recent Romers have proceeded clockwise around Greece, guided by Peter Hatlie and the other professors. Alternate sites have been visited from time to time, such as Thessaloniki, Meteora with its monasteries perched precipitously on phantasmagoric rock formations, Zeus's cult site Dodona, Nestor's "sandy" Pylos, Mistras (near ancient Sparta), and Thermopylae. Only one alternate site took: Lyle Novinski brought students to a monastery in Dafni, but after it was closed by an earthquake, Charlotte Sullivan, the art history teacher,

OPPOSITE, TOP
Margaret Crawford at the Cathedral of St. Andrew, Patras, Greece. *Anthony Mazur.*

OPPOSITE, BOTTOM
Daniel Bishop at the Cathedral of St. Andrew, Patras, Greece. *Anthony Mazur.*

3. Spring 1982: David Sweet informs me that he and Lyle Novinski kept the bottles of gin safe from the potted plants flying around the bar in the storm.

in 1985 suggested instead Hosios Loukas. There predominantly Roman Catholic students have begun to recognize the richness of the Orthodox tradition and the urgency of Christ's prayer "that they may all be one," as indeed Greek and Roman Christians are alike members of the One Body, the true Church.

The icons of the monastery are both familiar and strange; students know the Orthodox artistic tradition from Rome's oldest churches, yet of course Western art went in a naturalistic direction starting with Giotto, which can make the intensity of an icon's gaze almost unnervingly atavistic. The whole of Greece is both familiar and strange. However novel Rome may be to a child of American suburbia, it is a city—it is *the* city—of the West, in its ideals and outlook the defining locus of our civilization. To use an epic analogy, Aeneas is our great-grandfather, Odysseus only our great-uncle (if for both we add one or two hundred "greats"). That does mean that Odysseus is part of the family. Greece is not China or India or Arabia: we grow up still with Greek myths, learn at school of our indebtedness to Greece for philosophy and the natural sciences, and speak about politics with terms like "democracy" and "tyranny." But Diocletian's division of the empire in the third century AD between East and West not only fostered a religious divide in Europe between Orthodoxy and Catholicism but also reconfirmed the differences between Odysseus of the many ways and pious Aeneas, between the minds of Greece and Rome.

Even the terrain of Greece is startling and new. Upon disembarking in Patras, students find themselves between sea and mountain, and for ten days they are never far from both. While Italy's beauty is typically gentle and lovely, Greece's astounds and exhilarates as everything seems so immediate and distinct, as its features do not gently transition into one another but rather stand in almost dialectical contrast. Here is the beginning of philosophy, according to the philosopher of history Oswald Spengler, in the bold definition and differentiation of space that makes everything under the noonday sun—the sea, the mountains, the stony soil, the olive trees, the temples, the shining figures of the gods, the Forms—intelligible and beautiful, even things tragic, even the bleeding sockets of Oedipus, even Achilles covered in the gore of Trojan dead raging against his own mortality. One wonder after another calls out to the mind for contemplation. The mind habituated to contemplation then inevitably turns to the most fitting subject for it: the human face. In the museums of Greece, the *kouroi* and *kourai* statues do not possess the faces worn by time that students see at the Capitoline or Vatican museums. But in the Hellenic idealization of youthful beauty, they may see that faces are worth contemplating, including their own young faces, just as the sites of Greece make apparent that there is an intelligible order worth contemplating—as does the Rome semester curriculum. The overwhelming landscape proclaims that the world is titanic, splendid, and fascinating. Whether or not such a world is governed by anthropomorphic gods such as Homer's, without doubt its heroes must be godlike and ageless.

CITIZENS OF ROME

It is a curious turn of history that the Romantic philhellenism that inspires UD not only gave birth to modern Hellas but also gave a name to its people. Philhellenism inspired Westerners, such as Lord Byron, to join the Greeks in their war of liberation against the Ottoman Turks.[4] From that war, modern Hellas was born, and so the Greeks once again call themselves Hellenes. But for the previous 1,500 years, they had been Romers—*Romioi* to be precise. The people we call Byzantines never called themselves that, and for them Rome did not fall in 476 but in 1453; it had merely shifted capitals to Constantinople, the New Rome. Those Christians who bore the dual inheritance of Greece and Rome called themselves *Romioi*, a term that still connotes the exuberance and wildness of the Greek peasantry, of a Zorba.[5] Rome conquered Greece so that, to paraphrase Horace, Greece with its arts could conquer Rome—so that subsequently a kind of Rome then unimaginable could bring Hellenism to the world and Romanize it.

For Beatrice, the New Rome is not Constantinople but heaven. She tells Dante that he shall be "forever a citizen with me / of that Rome where Christ Himself is Roman." How can Dante have the temerity to conceive of the heavenly city as not the New Jerusalem but the New Rome? Maybe the reason is that the poet's heaven is not iconoclastic but iconodulic, one in which the human is to be venerated, and those human images not stylized but painted by a hand like Giotto's. In it are the faces of Saint Francis, Saint Bernard, and Saint Peter; the faces of Piccarda, Justinian, and Cacciaguida; the faces of old friends from Florence—Belacqua, Casella, Nino, and Forese—once they are freed from Purgatory; and, in the

4. On the back of the Church of the Transfiguration in Nafplion (where the sweet old Polish priest Father George has overloaded recent Romers with back issues of Catholic youth magazines) is the Apse of the Philhellenes honoring the Westerners who died fighting for Greek independence, including George Washington's cousin William Townsend Washington.

5. In Louis de Bernières's novel *Captain Corelli's Mandolin*, Dr. Iannis explains that "[e]very Greek…has two Greeks inside." The Hellene "believes in reason, he is the spiritual heir of Plato and Pythagoras," while the Romioi "will always compromise an ideal for self-interest, and they like getting drunk, and dancing and singing, and breaking bottles over each others' heads."

Empyrean, "the face that most resembles Christ" and finally His, "in its very color / painted with our likeness." These distinct faces from different times and lands all stand in relation to the Holy Face, playing in "ten thousand faces," to switch poets to Gerard Manley Hopkins, and remembered in 100,000 churches, prayer cards, and roadside shrines.

Here is one quirky take on the civilization that Christian Rome produced: from the comingling of Greek lucidity, Roman particularity,[6] and Christian belief in the Incarnation derives a sense that all sorts of faces and the world that foregrounds them are worth knowing and admiring. This sense of things may come most easily to Roman Catholics. Frederick Wilhelmsen, UD's beloved "Fritz," with no pretension could identify himself through the title of his collected essays as a *Citizen of Rome*. This exalted status, however, is not restricted on sectarian grounds: the Reformation is a development within Western Christendom, with certain aspects of *Romanitas* reaching their apogee in the Protestant nations, such as the rule of law and dutifulness. In *Eccentric Culture: A Theory of Western Civilization*, Remi Brague argues for an even more inclusive sense of Rome: contemporary multiculturalism could only have emerged in the West because of Rome's "secondarity," its indebtedness to primary sources outside of it, to the Greeks for their higher culture and to the Hebrews ultimately for their religion, from which follows an openness and inclusivity not so present in the other great civilizations. *Romanitas* does not exclude Hellenism, whereas the opposite may not be true.

Any UD Romer can, like Saul of Tarsus, claim to be a "Citizen of Rome." This citizenship confers a dignity that "Global Citizen" does not, as it affiliates one (literally "makes one a son," from the Latin *filius*) with the civilization that has achieved the richest sense of the human person and of human possibilities. There are many other blessings that the Rome semester provides, such as the potential to mature significantly through its challenges and to make lasting, deep friendships through the shared experience of foreign travel and a common intellectual life. Rome offers different gifts to different students needing different things. But for all students, the interplay of the books and the travel means the opportunity to be not merely a temporary resident but a Roman in mind and spirit. All those faces seen in Rome—in Piazza Navona and on the Cotral, peering down from Bernini's colonnade in Piazza San Pietro or out of a Caravaggio, on the pages of *King Lear*, *The Confessions*, and *The Phaedo*—and in the places to which Rome has brought its understanding, may transform the aspirations

6. The driving spirit of its pre-Olympian religion, in which every hill and grove was governed by a separate *numen*.

of students before their taking on adult responsibilities, while they are still considering how they should live their lives. Having studied so many faces and so many canvases, literal and metaphorical, the Romer is left to choose on which canvas to paint his or her own face.

A studying face, Diego Brand's, studying faces at the Capitoline Museum. *Stephen Henderson.*

INTERMEZZO. THE DOGS OF GREECE

Andrew Moran

Dogs don't get a very good press in the Bible. There is the one exception, Tobit, its most charming book, in which Tobias, on the road to unexpected blessings, a large inheritance and a lovely bride, is accompanied by not only the Archangel Raphael but also a dog. For the most part, however, biblical dogs are not very nice: they return to their own vomit; they lick sores; they lap up the blood of Ahab; they chow down on the corpse of Jezebel.

Greek dogs, however, were honored, and rightly so. Peritas was so loved by Alexander the Great, wrote Plutarch, that upon the dog's death he founded a city that he named after him. Only loyal Argos recognized the disguised Odysseus upon his return to Ithaca. Seeing the feebly wagging tail of the puppy he had left behind twenty years earlier, it now too old to move and abandoned on a dung heap by careless servants, much-enduring Odysseus shed a tear. UD students, too, have been on the verge of tears for Argos's descendants when saying goodbye to them in Athens, Delphi, and Nafplion. They had joined us for site tours, during which they often proved to be much more interesting than the professors; they had waited overnight at the doors of our hotels to greet us the next morning; and they had bid us adieu at our buses, at which sad partings I have remembered Saint Thomas More's hope that "may we all meet merrily in Heaven." For the dogs of Greece are not just loyal and endearing. They, the heirs of the ancient philosophers, model for the liberal arts student the life of the mind.

In fact, the "dog philosophers" composed one of the five great schools of classical philosophy, along with the Platonists, Aristotelians, Stoics, and Epicureans. The Cynics (from the Greek κύων, "dog") were called dogs as an insult because of their rejection of polite conventions out of a desire to live in accord with nature. But they made the name a badge of honor. For example, Diogenes, the most famous of the Cynics, the one who told Alexander to "get out of my light" and carried a lamp in daylight supposedly while "looking for an honest man," was disturbed to be applauded by the Corinthians after expounding on Hercules's virtue in cleaning the Augean stables. Such approval wouldn't do, and so, to reestablish the right relationship with them, he hiked up his tunic, squatted, and did a very doggy thing that quickly put a stop to

A descendent of Argos in Delphi engaging in the intellectual life.
Stephen Henderson.

Looking down from the Temple of Apollo in Delphi. *Patrick Goodman.*

their praise. The noun *cynic* thus entered our language pejoratively, as a term for someone whose attitude toward his fellow man is bitter and contemptuous. Despite the philosophical school's bad reputation, however, the second-greatest English playwright, Shakespeare's friend and rival Ben Jonson—by turns learned, irascible, elegant, goofy, profound, bawdy, and religious—identified himself as a Christian Cynic. In some of his plays, there is even a character clearly analogous to the author repeatedly associated with dogs. But how could the pagan insolence of a Diogenes have any appeal to a Christian intellect?

During the Spring 2016 Greece trip, I had my answer. Again, we made Hellene canine friends. And this time, one of them, Cinnamon, so called by the people of Nafplion for her color, joined us for drinks. We had seen her, free as the wind, bounding about town with a dumb chum, the two obviously well cared for by the townspeople but belonging to none of them. Eight of us were enjoying the cool night air at a bar on the central square, the Plateia Syntagmatos, with its lovely Venetian architecture, seven listening to a Philosophy-English double-major wax profound about some heavy topic. He—in retrospect, the most Jonsonian student I have ever taught—cut himself short when Cinnamon ambled up to join us. His eyes growing big, his mouth agape, his arms rising in the ecstasy of a Baroque saint, he finally could contain no longer his exultation. "PUUUUUUUPYYYYYYY!!!!!!!" He then embraced Cinnamon as if she were his lover and cooed sweet nothings into a floppy ear for an unconscionably long time, to the growing discomfort of everyone else at the table. Eventually, without ending the embrace, he looked up and—in sentences Ciceronian in their elegance and length, as lapidary as if they had been polished and re-polished in the study over a span of months with *Merriam-Webster* and Roget rarely left idle, their complexity in no way contravening their lucidity—began an encomium to the dogs of Greece, praising them for not only the usually celebrated virtues but also for the dignified and conscientious manner in which they attend to the promptings of nature, their thoughtful and generous practice of avoiding common pathways when taking care of their necessary business, in contrast to the geese back home in Georgia, whose slovenly ways mean that to walk from point A to point B one is required to pirouette like a ballerina. While I question his claim about their tidiness, in all other respects his praise for the dogs of Greece was just and so, too, his romantic ardor. I want to live with a Cinnamon dog. I could be happy the rest of my life with a Cinnamon dog.

UD students can't spend too much time chasing the moonlight with a Cinnamon dog due to the Greece trip's midnight curfew, but they should see in her roaming something akin to the intellectual life rightly lived, as the Cynics did in that of her ancestors. While we hope that our students have more respect for common hygienic practices than did the dog philosophers and than do the dogs, to understand what nature teaches does often require indifference to human custom. But the pursuit of truth is not a solitary exercise, as UD students know from the last two books of Aristotle's *Nicomachean Ethics*, on friendship; one still needs to run with a pack and nuzzle up to others who likewise stick their snouts into what smells most interesting. The life of the mind also demands energy: one has to shake a leg if one is going to leave one's mark. But dogged persistence is not enough. For more than anything, the life of the mind is dependent on a spirit of freedom. It's not in those canine *faux pas* that make us giggle but in the Greek dogs trotting around town—not like our dogs, cooped up in a house or bound by a leash, but free to pursue whatever their eyes, ears, nose, and tongue draw them to—that they reveal to us what it means to be a student of the liberal arts.

Surprisingly, some Christians appropriated the Cynics' model of doglike freedom, as Dr. Peter Hatlie pointed out to me after that trip. The holy fools of Eastern Orthodoxy sought to liberate themselves from worldly concerns through comically bizarre behavior and thus better devote themselves to Christ. Western Christendom, too, has Saint Francis of Assisi and Saint Philip Neri, who chased holiness while initiating play, his often unmuzzled antics (sometimes involving a dog!) ultimately serving to turn hearts and minds to the highest truth. But UD Romers already have their own experience of that playful freedom that enables one to approach the world with wonder and gratitude. The Greece trip is not going to bolster anyone's résumé, nor will it increase one's future earnings. The staging of scenes from Greek tragedies won't land anyone a role on Broadway; the students perform for their own and others' pleasure. Even the site tours are not requirements for any specific class: the students have already had their history and art history tests on Greek antiquity and won't get extra credit for running the race in Olympia. A morning in Delphi—ascending from the ruins of the cult of the mother goddess up to the Sacred Way, past the Temple of Apollo to the theater and the stadium, below the valley extending to the bay, all around mountains and mountains, with Parnassus and the Muses above one's head—is not of any practical importance. But it is glorious and teaches that creation, both divine and human, is worth sniffing into.

INTERMEZZO. GAMES AND TRADITIONS

Andrew Moran

Via del Pescaccio had its own traditions, such as drinking in the bombed ruins of the palazzo of Mussolini's mistress. There was also the speed-eating contest as young men would scarf their "Oliver Twist at the workhouse" portions, striving (usually in vain) to break the one-thousand-calorie barrier for the day by getting seconds before the food ran out. Very different traditions have emerged at Due Santi, as well as more of them. A home of our own has made it easier to pass down, semester to semester, games and customs. More importantly, the expanse from the umbrella pines to the back gate, from the villa to the vineyard, has meant that fresh legs—and fresh minds—can run free. Plato wrote in *The Laws* that young animals "leap and jump"—and those who know the demands but also the joys of the life of the mind want to jump higher. They understand why both ancient Greeks such as Lucian and Renaissance Humanists such as Thomas More held up as an ideal being *spoudogeloion*, mixing the ridiculous with the serious. For them, Due Santi is a place to play.

The soccer field hosts a tournament every November and April in which athletes show their stuff, novices trip and laugh, and professors recapture the glory

PREVIOUS
The match before the storm. *Steve Bisgrove.*

OPPOSITE, TOP
The torchbearer, Jordan Broussard, opens the G[r]eek Olympics, Spring 2019. *Anthony Mazur.*

OPPOSITE, BOTTOM
Joe Flynn as "Modest Aphrodite," Fall 2014. *Ivanna Bond.*

of youth and rack up major medical expenses. Teatro Due Santi no longer hosts a play every semester—the drama majors' productions were often brilliant but time-consuming—but the talent show remains a favorite. The *vendemmia*, the grape harvest, is a highlight of the fall, and after the closing convocation, students from both semesters bid Rome *arrivederci* at a bonfire. To the last day, some tradition is being upheld, some game played, bringing participants and spectators alike into a joyful unity.

But for delirious joy, nothing can compare to the G[r]eek Olympics. Credit goes to Travis Curtright, who as a Rome assistant in 1995 recognized that, with mid-terms having just ended and the big trip a day away, the students needed to celebrate their own Greek Olympics. A torchbearer (ideally physically coordinated) races down the rose path, a rainbow of bellowing toga-clad teams following. On the *mensa* field, they win abiding glory, and maybe a *forno* dinner, through contests specifically chosen for their hokeyness. These are the mortals' sacrifices to satisfy the gods watching from above—the professors on the terrace, for whom bottles of Peroni or spritzes substitute for ambrosia. Wayne Ambler, Zeus's lightning no match for his tennis racket, later introduced an ambiguity about its name that has never been resolved: aren't contestants in an egg-toss part of a *Geek* Olympics? The geekiest of all games, suggested by Laura Flusche in 2006, is now the culminating event: ten minutes, ten cans of shaving cream, a Romer's familiarity with classical statuary, one teammate in the role of art history professor explaining to the gods a statue's formal and historical importance, and at least one more willing to do anything for a laugh.

CHAPTER 6
THE YEARS I WORE EVERY HAT ON THE RACK—AND FOUND A FAMILY

VALLERY BERGEZ HRBACEK

Two and a half years after student life as a Fall 2011 Romer—the "Kinetic Class"—I returned to the bustling Fiumicino airport, this time shuffling two suitcases and two backpacks, hearing snippets of conversations in a language that I was anxious to understand. I buckled myself into the car and stared out the window at scenes that, while very close to me, felt ghostly. The car traveled at the speed of my own thoughts, one whizzing in front of another, memory after memory after memory.

When the car reached the Appia Nuova, we drove past sites that recalled memories even more vivid: the Top (once called the Dem), the charming white bar at the fateful Due Santi intersection, the stone archway with the imbedded icon of Saint Francis, and, at last, the view of the Eugene Constantin Campus, with its delicate pink walls and rows of vines bursting forth with life. After a few years, I had forgotten how beautifully the sun hits those walls, as if to wish you a good morning.

We turned through the sturdy gate and onto the driveway (which feels much more even and smooth when you are not on a large bus), and I peered outward and upward at the graceful umbrella pines, which seem to reach out and over you, building an archway to welcome you, for the first time and every time thereafter.

Returning to the Due Santi campus felt like a dream. My jet-lagged state partially explains this, but more importantly, I was returning to a place that had changed only slightly, while I had changed dramatically. And this place that had once been populated by one hundred classmates was now quiet and serene, the way it always seems during the summer. This dreamlike quality stayed with me for the entire first semester, lending a tinge of déjà vu to everything I saw and did.

What was so strange is that as an almost-twenty-two-year-old, I was here under entirely different circumstances: I was being paid instead of paying; I was working instead of studying; and I had my own room instead of one shared with two others. These different circumstances changed everything, and I strongly felt that change as I stepped out of the car for my first day of "work," my first day back in Rome and my first day in this new, intimidating, exciting, adventurous, joyful, difficult, lonely, enveloping stage of life.

These feelings of déjà vu became critical professionally, which is probably why the Rome Program typically hires UD graduates who have been through it themselves—and typically younger graduates who have been through the program more recently. Moments that would have annoyed or frustrated me actually brought sympathy, as I remembered that I, too, had once felt displaced and unsure of how to balance the thousand things being asked of me. Yet, ironically, as an RA, I frequently found myself in the same worn-out shoes, displaced and unsure of how to balance work and play.

When I reflect on this intense mélange of feelings, I realize that I never really "figured it out." I never really learned how to balance work and play; in fact, that became more difficult and more frustrating the longer I was there. As a student, you are thrust into these new experiences, and you just have to *do* the thing and live the life being asked of you. It is like learning how to swim by being thrown into the deep end: you have no choice but to flail your arms and legs until you get the hang of it and realize you are now floating. RAs are thrown into the deep end too; they are just also asked to help the more than one hundred other people in the deep end stay afloat.

The number of Rome assistants has fluctuated over the years—one, two, or three and, during my years, four, which makes for a nice balance of two men and two women (starting in 2017 the position was re-titled Rome coordinator, with one female RC and one male reporting to a director of student affairs). There is a long list of duties, encompassing everything from room preparations and textbook organization to medical responsibilities and chaplain's assistant. Before the students arrive, there is a two-week period of "pre-semester prep," during which this long list of duties is divvied up among the four RAs. Those duties are the RAs' principal projects throughout the semester. But "other tasks as assigned" becomes the most important, as this is the work that solidifies these graduates as a team that looks after one hundred or more college students on a high from traveling the world with their friends.

Jon Bird engaged in "other tasks as assigned." *Rome Campus Archives.*

Duty nights mean that there is a point-person at every moment of every day even a single student is on campus. The general schedule has two RAs on duty during the weekdays, with office hours from 9:00 a.m. to 5:00 p.m. After this, one RA is on duty until the following morning and has office hours from 9:30 p.m. to 11:30 p.m., and another RA is "on call," which means that (s)he must be within ten to fifteen minutes of campus in case of emergencies. All day Monday, all four RAs are on duty, and all work during event evenings—wine tastings, special meals, Cap Houses, and so on. During evening office hours, RAs generally just make themselves available to answer questions or help students with various needs. For each of the four "long weekends," one male and one female RA must stay on campus, and the other two may travel. Because all students must leave campus for Ten-Day, RAs also can travel that week, but one must stay for an extra day at the beginning and one must return a day early at the end. Finally, two RAs are on duty during Thanksgiving break, and the other two are on duty during Easter break; the two off-duty are free to travel. If this sounds complex and confusing, that is how it felt when it was first explained to me too.

These details are seldom known and understood outside the Rome faculty and staff circle, who honestly don't know the details to their full extent either. Even students, at the end of the semester, have not grasped what it is that "we even do" and whether or not we have free time. In their eyes, the lives of their RAs revolve around them, and I cannot comfortably say that they are wrong—RAs are there for the students.

The RAs live in the dormitory, which houses three staff apartments, two with kitchenettes. The fourth RA lives in half of a dorm-suite that has been converted into a one-bedroom apartment. In the basement, next to the laundry room, there is a cozy little one-bedroom apartment with a small kitchen, which some semesters a lucky RA can claim. These accommodations are more than enough, and having one's own space is a dramatic contrast to the tight-squeeze of so many Old Mill apartments we have shared and loved. The tough part of living in the dormitory is not our individual rooms, but the *dormitory itself*, with more than one hundred underclassmen for whom we work all day, most of whom assume that if they see you walking around without a clipboard, you must have time to take care of something for them.

The lack of privacy, largely a result of living so near the students, was perhaps the most difficult thing. I would daydream about what it must be like to see the clock hit 5:00 p.m. and know that your workday is truly over—that you can pack up your things, get in your car and drive *home*, leaving the frustrations of the workday at the office and unwinding in the comfort of your own space. I know that many people with "normal" nine-to-five jobs would call that sort of routine "mundane," but I often craved it: predictability, mundanity, a reliable routine. Instead, in my short walk from the RA office to my dorm room, I would get stopped every few steps to be asked questions by eager (sometimes desperate) students. I have heard other RAs say that this job is "all-consuming" or that it is "a lifestyle." These comments are accurate, as you almost live and breathe your job as you live in the place that you work and work in the place that you live.

Living in such close quarters, though, was pivotal to doing the job well. RAs were the eyes and ears for the whole program, the ones who knew if students were generally healthy and stable. We heard and saw more than we ever cared to hear or see, but that is why we were there. Students who struggled with deeper problems than the pressure of classes or the indecisiveness of whether to go to Prague or Madrid would not open up as readily if we were not so visible to them. RAs are like the protective older siblings, always keeping an eye on their younger brothers and sisters, constantly wondering and worrying. As a student, I never understood this aspect of the RAs' lives because I never needed them in any sort of serious way. As an RA, though, I understood that this is our most important responsibility, and it is not on the list of divided duties because every RA has 100 percent of the responsibility to keep an eye on these students—the bubbly ones, the shy ones, the excited ones, the nervous ones, the outcasts, the leaders, the depressed, the class clowns, and the rest. When I accepted the job offer, I may have known what this looked like on paper, but I quickly became aware of the weight of what this meant.

One of the first nights of my first semester, I was awakened by frantic knocks at my door and the shrill ring of my room phone. A few girls told me that some students had gotten lost and then mugged on their way home from a bar in Albano. I hurried down to the Cap Bar, where another student was trying to call one of the mugged students. The three were visibly scared. We weren't even through with orientation week; they were barely acclimated to living on a new campus, let alone living in a new country. At this point, I was joined by the other female RA, Ivanna Bond (in her first semester too). When one of the lost students was finally on the other line (the one male in the group), I grabbed the phone and tried to calm him down, my own heart beating fast. I realized that I had only one option: call a taxi for the students. But they had no idea where they were. It was late, and these small Italian towns have little if any street lighting. The student had no idea what to look for, and I didn't even know where to begin. Ivanna and I grabbed a map of the town and did our best to ask the right questions. The students continued walking until they came across a visible street sign. We eventually figured out their approximate location, called a taxi, and waited for their return. Thankfully they got home safely, although they did have bruises and scratches. They were shaky and frightened and vowed never to walk home from the bar again—of course, they did. We later learned that the intoxicated students had not been mugged but had merely suffered a bad fall.

In the semesters that followed, situations like this came up frequently—students getting lost, students in major accidents, students having mental breakdowns. One semester, a nervous student came to the office to tell me about a friend she was worried about; she thought she might have an eating disorder. I kept an eye on the student, noticed the same behavior her friend had told me about, and finally sat down to talk with her. I scheduled counseling appointments with our counselor in Rome, walked her to the counselor's office and checked in with her constantly.

There were less dramatic cases too, typically involving a student being intoxicated. Sometimes the level of intoxication was cause for legitimate concern. Here is why there are rules on the Due Santi campus—rules that, in the students' eyes, are strict and unfair, but they exist to ensure their safety and well-being. We say this repeatedly

The Rome coordinators brook no nonsense. *Stephen Henderson.*

in the initial meeting about student life matters, but it never sinks in as we hope. Enforcing these rules is a challenge. When you punish a student, you risk damaging any rapport you had with him or her. That can hurt the ego, but more importantly, it can make trust more difficult. RAs constantly toe this delicate line of how to respond to students breaking the rules. Being a disciplinarian is much more difficult when you are also called on to be an older sibling.

It is in the "older sibling role" that you find the crux of the RAs' responsibilities. While a suffering student is never a good thing, the intimate conversations shared with suffering students were moments of true friendship, completely affirming why you love what you do. Even in the most difficult of cases, knowing that a fragile person was looking to you as a mentor and entrusting his worries and fears and pains to you was fulfilling. As an RA, you have been there before, either in those same worn-down shoes or among others who wore them. There are growing pains that come with the Rome semester, and we experienced them when we were students too, and not that long ago. And little do the students realize that we are dealing with our own growing pains as RAs. The transition from the set patterns of undergraduate life to the flux of post-graduate life is unnerving, and we deal with this an ocean away from our peers and family members. We miss engagements, weddings, birthdays, funerals. We, too, are exhausted by the semester's schedule; the ones who give the wake-up calls must wake up earlier. We may enforce rules that the students would prefer not to have and may be more experienced travelers, but we are also at a difficult place in our lives. Conversations in which students acknowledge their vulnerabilities, admittedly more frequent on the female side of the office, created a camaraderie, as the RAs are at a vulnerable time as well. That glimpse into our common situation kept me grounded and focused.

Lest it sound like everything the RAs do is deeply meaningful, I should note some of our mundane duties: drive to the Italian version of Costco to fill up a car with boxes of supplies for the Cap Bar and the infinite number of *forno* dinners we cooked for students; take keys to the tiny local hardware store for copies; drive to and from the train station to pick up or drop off seminarians or faculty who lived in the city; and lug mini-fridges up to the rooms that paid for them. One time, due to an excess of bird poop in Shakespeare Alley from a group of relentless sparrows, Peter Hatlie, the director of the Rome Program, and Fabio Cinalli, the facilities manager, asked the RAs to construct curtains made of long, plastic beads that would hang from the entrance to Shakespeare Alley and from the opposite entrance to a storage space by the RA offices. These curtains would supposedly prevent the sparrows from flying through the entryways. They were unbelievably tedious to make. There were small metal prongs with tiny loops on either side, and we had to push one of the loops into one end of the long bead, push a new prong into the other end, add a bead and so on and so on and so on. They took ages to make. It was the kind of repetitive task that made your thumbs sore and your wrists in need of a stretch every few minutes. Within a couple of days of the curtains (incongruously, garishly bright red) being hung, individual beads had fallen off, strands of beads were getting tangled with other strands and the curtains would snap backward and hit the students who tried to pass through. Ironically, the curtains ended up trapping the sparrows *within* Shakespeare Alley: they made their way in but never learned how to get back out. Not only was Shakespeare Alley filled with poop again, but sparrows were constantly darting out of dark corners and into the faces of the innocent. We heard shrieks at all hours. After a few weeks, Peter and Fabio surrendered, and the now-mangled bead curtains that had taken days to put together were tossed in the trash.

Whether because of serious situations or bead curtains, there was always a need to get away and recharge. This is why most RAs travel whenever we can, seeing cities we never dreamt we'd see. Romers often talk about the cities they wish they had had the chance to visit; RAs can go back and make up for it. In my two years, I saw the stone spires of Oxford, the snowy mountains of Salzburg, the windmills of Holland, the churches of Avignon, the minarets of Istanbul, the markets of Lucca, the sands of Split, and the craters of Mount Etna—and that is not an exhaustive list. This is the life—catching trains, exploring new cities, and eating strange food—that I know people envision when they ask me dreamily with starry eyes, "How *was* it?" This is the Romantic image—the young, impressionable, adventurous nomad—that people stamp on the forehead of the RA. But these nomads still return to their bedrooms in a dormitory, trying to catch up on sleep for the busy workweek ahead.

Yet that return after some time away is beautiful, as it reflects how truly Rome, and Due Santi in particular, has become one's home. Students feel this, too, but the sense of "Rome as home" is stronger and deeper for the RAs. It is hard to talk about without sounding like we took it for granted, but we do not always stop to stare wide-eyed at the façade of St. Peter's, the slow-moving waters of the Tiber passing beneath the Ponte Sisto, or the Vespas revving around sharp cobblestone street corners in Trastevere—not because we do not care or are "over it" but because these scenes have become normal for us, in much the same way that the surroundings of our stateside homes are normal. I do not think this shows a numbness or a disregard; I think that is what it means to have found a new home. And RAs really have.

Even more astonishing, cities like Delphi, Florence, Athens, and Venice become similar to the vacation spots that your family returns to over and over again. You come to know these cities so well that you know by name the man who owns that tiny pottery

Theresa Guin, Stephen Henderson, and Ben Gibbs lead the ever-enjoyable Monday Night Meeting. *Vasile Chiriac.*

shop in Nafplion; you know the best place to get a panino in Florence; you recognize when a bar in Athens has changed its décor. (However, no matter how many times you have been to Venice, it is still easy to find yourself caught at a dead-end after crossing a canal.)

All of these things provide comfort and familiarity to the flux of the RA life. You are constantly kept on your toes, but there is grounding and stability in these moments and these places so well understood. There is confidence in knowing that if and when a student is seriously hurt and needs to go to the hospital, you know how to drive there and communicate with the Italian medical staff; or if part of the group gets separated during an Art and Architecture trip in Rome, you can lead them back; or when the semester gets threatened with the fear of terrorism (as it did after the Paris attack in the fall of 2015), the leaders of the Rome Program will make the best possible decisions and you will stand by them; or when you make a mistake, the Rome staff will stand by you because we are all on the same team.

To describe the Rome staff and faculty as a team, however, still falls massively short. When Ryan calls Ivanna and me in the

Vallery Bergez and Joe Hrbacek, on their engagement. *Paulina Martín.*

middle of the night to come watch his daughter while he and Ellen drive to Rome to give birth to their new baby, he cannot be called a teammate. When someone in Ivanna's family passes away and the student life staff comes together so that she can fly to the States for the funeral, we are not just teammates. When I find out that a friend has been diagnosed with cancer, and the Rome staff offers prayers and comfort at every turn, we are not just "on the same team."

During Holy Week of my final semester, Joe and I got engaged. The ring was too big, and I was too bashful to announce it right away anyway, so we decided to wait a few days to tell everyone. But I wanted to get the ring re-sized as soon as possible. I snuck out of the RA offices, asked Silvia and Alessandra in the Business Office if I could speak with them privately, and took the ring out of my pocket, grinning. They squealed and embraced me and jumped up and down as if they were my sisters. Immediately, they were each on their cellphones calling uncles and cousins and second cousins and friends and friends of friends to see who could re-size the ring for me. I ended up taking it to this small shop in Marino owned by a family member of Alessandra, and he seemed as elated for me as if I had been his own relative.

Eventually, we told staff and faculty one on one. We popped open bottles of prosecco and celebrated our happy news. One day, Nino and Nuccia, the *mensa* chefs, invited Joe and me to their home. Nino told me with a wink that he cooked my favorite: *gnocchi all'amatriciana*. Toward the end of the lunch, Nuccia passed over a gift bag that held a beautiful silver Italian-made candlestick. It was a wedding gift, given to us by the two people who had been making us meals for the past two years, sweetly (Nuccia) or gruffly (Nino) encouraging us as we strained to find the right Italian words to express what we meant.

Joe and I were celebrated and congratulated over and over again. We even got a standing ovation when we shared the news with the Spring 2016 Rome class during a Monday Night Meeting. It was such a joyful time, yet I was also so sad that my family and friends could not celebrate with us; I wished so badly that we could share our joy with them over more than a phone line.

Fast-forward to November, to the day when Joe and I got married, and I again felt that sense that people were missing—that family was missing. This time, though, it was our Due Santi family. This time, it was those teammates who had become so much more than teammates. The people who supported us so generously at our engagement were now the ones on the other end of the telephone line. Missing these people in this way made them feel more like family than they had ever felt before. But some Due Santi family were there. The Rome chaplain, Monsignor Fucinaro, flew across the ocean to celebrate the wedding Mass, assisted by two priests who as seminarians we had met in Rome. Ivanna and Mike Pitstick, another RA, also flew in from Rome and were the lectors. A bond that brings people across an ocean to witness your wedding is more than a bond between co-workers or teammates.

When I accepted the job as an RA, I had never even considered my relationships with the other people living on the Eugene Constantin Campus beyond the other three RAs, and even then, I just considered those relationships because I knew we would be working so closely together. Looking back on my two years, the most influential thing that happened to me as an RA was the building up of this collection of people, all there for work, into a family.

There is Peter, *Il Capo*, the kind of boss who jokes that Joe never asked his permission to marry me yet stands in front of students, faculty, and staff with a quiet, composed confidence as he informs everyone of the measures he is taking to ensure our safety after the Paris terrorist attacks. There are Ryan and Ellen, the couple who let us invade their home nearly every night for hours of Settlers of Catan and gin and tonics and share tears as we load our luggage into the taxi on our final morning in Rome. There is the chaplain, Monsignor Fucinaro, who gives homilies that push you to be better and hosts you for a four-course homemade meal because it brings him joy to love others so generously. There is the assistant chaplain, Father Brown the astronomer, a patient listener and wise man who has every right to brag about how intelligent he is and how cool his job is but never, ever does. There are Silvia and Ale, who, in the midst of their immense operational responsibilities, always take the time to ask you about your day and actually care to hear your response. There are Nino and Nuccia, who save extra plates of your favorite dishes and recommend restaurants in the city for date nights. There is Isa, the gorgeous woman with an eye for detail as she tidies everything and prepares rooms for guests, always acknowledging you with some kind of a compliment. There are Fabio, Tiziano, and Giovanni, the quintessentially Italian men who keep campus as sharp and breathtakingly beautiful as it is and who make us espresso of the highest quality and chuckle when we sincerely offer to make it for them instead. There are all of the faculty members, who pick us up from the airport after a trip and share drinks with us as we revisit memories of a Greece trip on a ferry, whose children we babysit and birthdays we celebrate.

I miss the Eternal City, with its countless churches tucked between storefronts, *pizza al taglio* windows with fresh, oily slices, and charming cobblestone streets with greenery crawling all along the walls. But what I miss and crave most from my time as an RA are the long meals in the *salone*, celebrating holidays or achievements or special announcements. I miss playing silly games with the little children, hiding behind plants and doorways. I miss the genuine laughter as another bottle of wine is opened and poured into glasses. I miss being completely unaware of the hours and minutes as we just enjoy one another's company, and I miss the shared looks of exhaustion as we suddenly realize how many hours have passed since we began.

People always ask me, "How *was* it?" I think of all of these things: the highs and lows and frustrations and joys of what it was like to wear so many different hats as a recent graduate working and living with more than one hundred undergraduates in a different country for two years. What always bubbles to the surface, though, and I know that this will always be the case, is not the job itself, but the people I became close enough with to call my family.

INTERMEZZO. THE CHAPLAINCY

Andrew Moran

Save for the willfully obtuse and the aggressively indifferent, a semester spent reading Aeschylus, Thucydides, Plato, Augustine, and Shakespeare will make one more thoughtful about human purpose and destiny. The city of Rome complements this growing thoughtfulness about ultimate things, most obviously because it is the city of Peter, Paul, and other martyrs, as well as John Paul and other popes, and Baroque churches dramatically and polychromatically proclaiming the glory of God. While an excellent liberal education does not necessarily lead to becoming religious or more religious, most Romers, especially the Catholics, do grow in desire for understanding of their faith and in commitment to it. But texts and artwork are not enough to explain the spiritual flowering that occurs on the Rome campus. The semesters have continuously produced blessings because of priests who have dedicated themselves to the spiritual welfare of the students.

The tradition began with Father Damian Fandal, OP, the Rome Program's first director and first chaplain, one of the great men in the university's history, as older alumni know. A number of chaplains have been Cistercian monks from the Abbey of Our Lady of Dallas, including Father Gilbert Hardy and the first at Due Santi, Father James Lehrberger. In the 2000s, priests from the Society of Our Lady of the Most Holy Trinity (SOLT) staffed the chaplaincy, such as Father Mark Byrne. But at Due Santi, the chaplains have primarily been Americans working in the Curia, first Monsignor Nevin Klinger and then Monsignor James Conley. The university took joy in the latter's subsequent elevation to auxiliary bishop of Denver and then to bishop of Lincoln, Nebraska.

After their day jobs at the Vatican, these chaplains have endured the traffic out of Rome to get to their night jobs at Due Santi, where they have heard confessions, said Mass, dined with the students, and been a friendly face around campus. After years of assisting his friend Monsignor Conley, Monsignor Thomas Fucinaro, undersecretary of the Congregation for the Sacred Liturgy and director of the Villa Strich (the house for American priests working at the Vatican), took on this role in 2005. Whether it be presiding over the wine tasting, securing tickets to a papal Mass, or taking students

ABOVE Mass on top of Mount Parnassus, celebrated by Greece trip chaplain Father Matthew Rolling, Spring 2019. *Anthony Mazur.*

LEFT Monsignor Thomas Fucinaro. *Peter Burleigh.*

out to dinner after they had served the poor at the Missionaries of Charity's soup kitchen, he has for fifteen years been an integral part of campus life. Father David Brown, SJ, an astronomer at the papal observatory in Castel Gandolfo, joined him in 2010. Their personalities differ, but they are one in their service to the students. The gratitude for that care is hinted at in all the frequent flier miles they rack up during their vacations back in the United States, flying around the country to preside at the weddings and baptize the children of alumni.

Father David Brown, SJ. *Anthony Mazur.*

INTERMEZZO. CLASS NICKNAMES

Andrew Moran

From conversations at Old Mill and alumni reunions, it seems that every Romer assumes that his class was the winner of at least one superlative—as the most interesting, intelligent, or wildest group ever. Such arguments are on the level of whether Babe Ruth, Ted Williams, or Willie Mays was the greatest baseball player of all time—much fun to hash out but impossible to resolve. But since 2006, Romers can at least boast of an ontological reality about their semesters that can never be disputed or lost: the class nickname has given them an identity as immutable as the Platonic forms.

Dr. Peter Hatlie is not given to flattery or cheap sentiment, but he, like the other professors in the fall of 2006, found that semester an especially happy one and admired its students. Not only did the semester go smoothly, and not only were the students as a whole fun and good-natured, but a group of them, led by the young women known as "the Pixies," went out of their way to make everyone, both other students and faculty, feel welcome through hosting *forno* parties and through various small kindnesses. Without intending to start a tradition, Dr. Hatlie in his speech at the closing ceremony expressed his affection by dubbing theirs "The Joyous Class." Nor did Dr. Andrew Moran, who gave the closing speech the following spring, have any thought of a new tradition. But as their Fall Romer friends had been given a nickname, he thought that he should bestow one on the Spring Romers, a name suggested to him by Dr. Joseph Stibora: "The Providential Class," a pleasant euphemism to remind them of all the dumb luck that had graced their semester. It was Dr. Hatlie then the following fall who made what might have been a quirk of the 2006–7 school year into one of Due Santi's most cherished traditions.

Students now arrive in Rome having heard of the tradition and at the closing ceremony are often even anxious to know how they will be immortalized. Some semesters they leave for the United States feeling like the heroes of Elysium if given a name that unambiguously honors them, such as "The Crusher Class" (they crushed it). "The Royal Class" acclaims the Spring 2020 students for their noble and generous response to the coronavirus pandemic, which ended their semester early. Sometimes students receive a nickname whose layers of irony provoke a smile and an acknowledgement that the semester had both highs and lows. Every semester, the final speech is an occasion for laughs, memories, and thoughtfulness about the great blessing that is the Rome semester. Following is a list of the nicknames. Occasionally, a professor about to return to the United States delivers the speech and names the class, as is noted in parentheses following; otherwise, the nicknames were given by Dr. Hatlie.

Fall 2006	Joyous
Spring 2007	Providential (Dr. Andrew Moran)
Fall 2007	Effortless
Spring 2008	Inscrutably Loyal
Fall 2008	(none given)
Spring 2009	Rainbow
Fall 2009	Chiaroscuro
Spring 2010	Angry Gods
Fall 2010	All or Nothing
Spring 2011	Blessed
Fall 2011	Kinetic
Spring 2012	Class for All Seasons
Fall 2012	Uncharacteristic
Spring 2013	Crusher
Fall 2013	Common
Spring 2014	Hands-On (Dr. Andrew Osborn)
Fall 2014	Crescendo
Spring 2015	Night and Day
Fall 2015	Pour L'Amour
Spring 2016	Almost Perfect
Fall 2016	Ap[p?]ian Way (Dr. Moran)
Spring 2017	Delphine
Fall 2017	Live and Learn
Spring 2018	Heliotrope (Dr. Kathryn Davis)
Fall 2018	Unquenchable
Spring 2019	Wayfaring (Dr. Philip Gonzalez)
Fall 2019	Extra Credit
Spring 2020	Royal

CHAPTER 7
"L'INFINITO"

A Sentimental Journey into the Four Seasons of the Rome Campus

Silvia De Simone

"*L'infinito*"

Sempre caro mi fu quest'ermo colle,
e questa siepe, che da tanta parte
dell'ultimo orizzonte il guardo esclude.
Ma sedendo e mirando, interminati
spazi di là da quella, e sovrumani
silenzi, e profondissima quiete
io nel pensier mi fingo, ove per poco
il cor non si spaura. E come il vento
odo stormir tra queste piante, io quello
infinito silenzio a questa voce
vo comparando: e mi sovvien l'eterno,
e le morte stagioni, e la presente
e viva, e il suon di lei. Così tra questa
immensità s'annega il pensier mio:
e il naufragar m'è dolce in questo mare.

"The Infinity" (English)

Always to me beloved was this lonely hillside
And the hedgerow creeping over and always hiding
The distances, the horizon's furthest reaches.
But as I sit and gaze, there is an endless
Space still beyond, there is a more than mortal
Silence spread out to the last depth of peace,
Which in my thought I shape until my heart
Scarcely can hide a fear. And as the wind
Comes through the copses sighing to my ears,
The infinite silence and the passing voice
I must compare: remembering the seasons,
Quiet in dead eternity, and the present,
Living and sounding still. And into this
Immensity my thought sinks ever drowning,
And it is sweet to shipwreck in such a sea.

Giacomo Leopardi (1798–1837)

Cornflowers.
Vasile Chiriac.

Although I had been living just a stone's throw away from the Eugene Constantin Campus, I had never heard of it until my interview for the position of office manager. What were the "hedgerows" that had kept me from seeing and enjoying "the endless space…the silence, and the peace"? The *physical* hedgerow was, of course, the main gate. When closed, one is cut off from the students' laughter, the buildings, and the colors of the beautiful plants and flowers. But upon entering, my first image was of an ancient Roman aristocratic woman, softly lying on a triclinium between the hills of the Castelli Romani, Lake Albano, and the Papal Palace, noble and simple: the olive trees and the vineyard on your right, the avenue of huge pine trees leading you to a beautiful sunset through which you see Rome at the right distance, and the villa on the left whose color is enhanced by the light of the evening and seems to sail off into that Roman sunset.

The *mental* hedgerow was my restricted world of family life, community events, and, of course, the undeniable dominance of the capital city, whose magnificence overshadows every other reality. It was so interesting and exciting to realize that such a garden of flowers was, in reality, a garden of souls, made up of students who were experiencing a sort of Grand Tour of the modern age: the rite of passage, the opportunity for great cultural, social, and moral learning and, above all, an occasion for personal growth—experiences that last a lifetime.

I don't want to sound too romantic, but I have always loved the comparison between children and flowers. You water both daily with love and watch them bloom. This reflects what the Rome Program does. Like patient gardeners, professors, assistants, and staff cultivate "taking care," one of the most sublime attitudes of the human soul. Having a capacity for taking care of somebody else is important not only for the receivers of the care but also for the caregivers, who abandon their ego and devote themselves to others without expecting anything in exchange.

Cicero, in a letter to Varro, left an insight that will never grow old: "*Si hortum in bibliotheca habes, deerit nihil*" ("If you have a garden and a library, you have everything you need"). Due Santi has both: flowers and plants, books and programs, which are, according to their nature and purpose, made for projecting forward and teaching us day by day how to enlarge our visions and horizons.

This is why my reflections in this chapter will be both on the Rome campus students and plants, a sort of sentimental journey among the four seasons of the Rome Program and of its gardens. Let us take this occasion to switch off our computers or cellphones and turn to an application that is not virtual: a walk into an unpolluted and real world made of beautiful fields, true colors and shapes, history, art, literature, religion, human beings, laughs, life, and personal considerations. I hope that it will be "sweet to shipwreck in such a sea."

ARRIVAL: THE TRIUMPHAL PROCESSION

Nothing behind me, everything ahead of me, as is ever so on the road.
—*Jack Kerouac,* On the Road

As soon as you enter the Rome Campus, the road is flanked by the umbrella pines that lead you to the Business Office, and if you turn your back and face the main gate again, you will notice that the big pine alley continues for another one hundred meters across the road. It's really nice to think that, before the Via dei Ceraseti was asphalted, these beautiful, ancient, typical Mediterranean trees used to shade this long walking path in its entirety, from east to west, from dawn to sunset. Their treetops, spread out in the shape of an umbrella, represent a fit of enthusiasm heavenward; their irrepressible roots, a burst of generosity toward the earth, make one feel closer to infinity and down to earth at the same time. Via dei Ceraseti derives from the Latin *cerasa*, cherry, a sign that cherry trees were planted in ancient times in an area transverse to the Via Appia Antica, the Appian Way, queen of the Roman long roads.

The legion of triumphant students usually arrives from Fiumicino Airport to our campus in three or four buses. Part of their American life has been squeezed into two big suitcases. It looks like they are saying: My decision to come abroad is the best I could possibly make, but still my journey is filled with uncertainty, so I want to bring as much of home as possible with me.

Upon the students' arrival, my thoughts go immediately to the Italian composer Ottorino Respighi and his *Pini di Roma. The Pines of Rome* consists of four movements, each depicting pine trees located in different areas in Rome at different times of the day. The fourth movement, "Pines of the Appian Way," portrays pine trees along the Appian Way in the misty dawn as a triumphant legion advances along the Via Appia in the rising sun. Listen to this last movement and consider it the soundtrack of the beginning of this Roman experience: the organ seems to reproduce the ground trembling under the footsteps of the army, and the trumpets announce that the consular army has arrived at its destination in triumph. Upon their arrival on campus, students are received and welcomed by our Rome coordinators and immediately plunged into the new Rome Campus life: an orientation tour, health and safety presentations, program expectations, dinner on the shores of Lago Albano, *permessi di soggiorni* applications, a fundatory (fun and mandatory) scavenger hunt in Rome, and a wine tasting.

As a woman and mother, I would like to dedicate the azalea flower to our Rome students and welcome them to my country by wishing the happiness and serenity that this flower represents. The azalea comes originally from the Far East and is a feminine flower, not only for the rose color of the petals but also for its meaning. It is the symbol of motherly love and represents temperance, a virtue taught by all mothers to their children when facing different experiences in life. Maybe it's just a coincidence, but the azalea flowers have found their natural habitat on the Rome campus. They perfectly grow and flower in its microclimate all year long, inhabiting pots on the walls near the main gate. They are a true explosion of color, and every time our florists see them, they always say how amazing they are. "The Royalty of the Garden" (the azalea's epic epithet) has inspired many poets and painters; hopefully its blooms will introduce royalty to the heart of our students.

THE *VENDEMMIA*: THE VINEYARD AND THE "QUEEN'S PATH"

Everything changes according to the window from which reality is observed.
–Banana Yoshimoto

Wine is not just fun; it's a complex blend of nature, art, culture, and science. Each drop of wine has taken sunshine, rain, and biological nutrients and is the result of laborious work, patience, and professional testing to achieve the final product. It is with a touch of pride that I tell people that the University of Dallas in Rome has its own vineyard and produces its own wine. The vineyard is relatively small compared to the extensive local and famous Castelli vineyards but has a charm of its own, growing two different varieties of grapes, Merlot and Cabernet Sauvignon. The focus is on quality, not quantity.

Nowadays, it is very hard to establish a dialogue with nature. Our life is becoming more hectic by the minute, and in addition, our attention is increasingly caught only through the intermediation of electronic media or a technological eye. We are getting more and more distracted and less interested in the real world. Who among us has never found himself or herself staring at the satellite map of our phones, which reproduce the natural landscape we have in front of us?

The *vendemmia* (the grape harvest) is a fascinating experience that the Fall Romers enjoy to the fullest. The countryside in September has the typical colors of the harvest—leaves are turning to golden and red shades—and temperatures are pleasantly mild. The students gather in the morning and have an introduction to the vineyard before beginning. They start collecting grapes and then stomp them with their feet, adorning themselves with grape leaf garlands, singing and dancing among the rows of wines, making everyone's heart smile with their cheerfulness. Being part of a thousands-year-old tradition is magical, the memories indelible.

Both in life and in nature, colors are everything to me. And in the canvas of our vineyard, the protagonist is not only the intriguing shade of purple grapes or the brightness of the leaves but also the impudent red of the roses that, like fireworks, light up the path between two rows of vines and divide the vineyard into two sections. Every time I walk that path, I feel like a queen among the queen of all flowers, thinking how blessed I am to work in a place like this. I feel ravished by this flamenco dance of roses, whose powerful color is reflected everywhere.

However, the real reason roses are planted in the vineyard is much less romantic than one might think. Roses are susceptible to the same type of fungal disease as

ABOVE The rose path in the vineyard. *Michael Housewright.*

is the grapevine. Therefore, they may serve as a warning to the vineyard manager that he needs to take action soon or the grapevines will be infected. If roses in the vineyard are healthy, it means that the vines are growing fine.

OPPOSITE, TOP "Even when seen from near, the olive shows / A hue of far away" (Wilbur, "Grasse: The Olive Trees"). *Vasile Chiriac.*

OPPOSITE, BOTTOM Due Santi in winter. *Stephen Henderson.*

THE WHISPERS OF THE OLIVE TREES

The earth has its music for those who will listen.
–Reginald Vincent Holmes

Next to the vineyard, there is a small piece of land the university acquired a few years ago. It's a sort of terrace full of olive trees that reminds me of the olive tree paintings by Vincent van Gogh. His paintings of olive trees and olive pickers demonstrate the relationship between man and nature and the connection to the divine through one's interaction with nature.

20

Listen to the whispers of these typical Mediterranean trees. Whispers of wisdom: Athena was the goddess of justice and wisdom and protector of arts and literature. Her sacred animal was the owl, and the olive tree was one of her most recognized symbols. Whispers of peace: Eirene, personification of peace, daughter of Zeus and Themis, was always depicted in art as a beautiful young woman with an olive branch in her hand. In periods of war, the messengers of peace held olive branches in their hands. Whispers of hope: In the Old Testament, a dove returns with an olive branch to the ark, announcing the end of the flood and a new hope to people. Whispers of strength: Hercules managed to kill the Cithaeron lion, which was ravaging the countryside, using only his own hands and a wooden stake from a wild olive tree. Whispers of light: The olive oil was used as lighting oil and therefore considered a source of light (Homer called it "liquid gold"). Whispers of health: Democritus believed a diet of honey and olive oil could allow a man to live to one hundred. Whispers of democracy: The olive branch figures prominently on the seal of the United States of America.

THE MARY GARDEN AND THE SUMMER GROUPS

Au milieu de l hiver, j apprenais enfin qu il y avait en moi un été invincible
("In the midst of winter, I found that there is within me an invincible summer").
—Albert Camus, Noces / L été

The Mary Garden is a small, secluded space behind the villa, far from activity. At each side, the statue is surrounded by two flowerbeds of what seem to be a sort of tropical, evergreen plants, with large and round green leaves, as well as by pale yellow roses, a traditional symbol of friendship, which seem to say, "Thanks for being you, and thanks for being with us." This sacred place makes you feel at peace; you smile, and it seems that you receive from this harmony another smile in return, like a continual spiritual exercise for your soul. The statue's outstretched arm is the typical gesture that we usually make when we welcome guests into our house.

Each summer, we welcome summer groups, very different from one another: the School of Ministry, Ripon College, the summer undergraduates, Shakespeare in Italy, Latin in Rome and, recently, Rome and the Catholic Church. Different programs, different students and professors. The time they spend on campus is limited, but the intensity and importance of their programs are undoubtable. For the summer groups, I have chosen lavender. The name of this plant comes from the Latin *lavare*, "to wash,"

The Mary Garden behind the Villa Gabriella. *Rome Campus Archives.*

since it is frequently used in baths and helps purify and calm the body and spirit. On first glance, the plant alone may present understated characteristics. Its foliage is skimpy, its flowers grow lanky and its pastel colors, gray-green and gray-violet, are so soft that you can hardly see when the buds bloom. But how enchanting it is being in a garden of lavender on a sunny day in summertime. In numbers, lavender plants create a beautiful Mediterranean ambience. And lavender plants become so versatile that they can be used to create perfumes, potpourris, sachets, soaps, teas, jellies, or cosmetics. Lavender transports us to a different world, where the clean and penetrating fragrance and the sight of the purple color inspire intense and sweet thoughts. I dedicate lavender's meaning to all the students and professors coming to the Rome Campus during summer time: your remembrance is my only happiness.

SPRINGTIME: THE EVERLASTING RENEWAL OF THE ROME CAMPUS

Perchè io stessa ero diventata un fiore, io stessa avevo un gambo e una linfa
("Because I myself had become a flower, I myself had a stem and a sap").
–Alda Merini

Springtime is my favorite season on the Rome Campus. The weather is never too hot or too cold; the sky always seems to be the perfect blue. Birds tweet, and you can open the windows and smell the freshness of air and grass; all the flowers are blooming, and the green of the trees and grass are never so bright. It is a time of phenomenal renewal; the earth awakens and explodes with new life.

A springtime walk takes one past the dedication plaques scattered about campus. As spring can represent the symbolic start of new projects, I want to dedicate the first burst of campus spring flowers, so beautiful and fragrant, to the lives and people on the plaques and the continuation of a project that is still ongoing, the Due Santi Campus.

IN LOVING MEMORY OF LIEUTENANT ERIC A. HAMM, '88, U.S. NAVY
Eric, beloved UD alumnus from the Hamm-Papania clan, died in a non-hostile incident in the Sea of Japan at the age of twenty-eight on October 14, 1994. Like the cypresses that are located near the gate, he represents for me the sentinel and the guardian of the Rome Campus. His flower is the magnolia, which attracts good luck and was usually planted near every house to wish strength to its foundations.

THIS VILLA WAS FOR MANY YEARS THE CHERISHED FAMILY HOME OF RENZO PIGA AND EDYTHE KOLLERSTROM
You met Renzo and Edythe and their family in Greg Roper's chapter. Their flower cannot be anything except the hydrangea (in Italian, *ortensia*). The originally Chinese hydrangea, named by the eighteenth-century naturalist Philibert Commerson for his love, Hortense Lapeaute, pays homage with its many colors to ever-changing human love; it grows near the villa in which Renzo and Edythe lived happily together for so many years.

THIS CAMPUS WAS CONSTRUCTED IN GREAT PART THANKS TO THE HARD WORK, DEDICATION, AND CARE OF RANDY LEE IRLBECK
The campus *forno* creates a warm and friendly atmosphere and is a place of fun and laughter, especially during those evenings when the sunset burns across the Roman skyline. Students and staff entertain themselves by throwing homemade pizza

"Those green-robed senators of mighty woods, / Tall oaks, branch-charmed by the earnest stars, / Dream…all night without a stir" (Keats, *Hyperion*). *Vasile Chiriac.*

parties or by smoking, baking, grilling, roasting, and barbecuing delicacies. Every time I have a *forno* dinner with campus staff, friends, or guests, I silently raise my glass for a toast to Randy. The big Holm oak near the *forno* is the plant I wish to dedicate to him—a strong, vigorous, and evergreen tree that surrounds and enriches our beautiful Mediterranean land and overlooks our outdoor oven. The Holm also represents long life, perseverance, dignity, majesty, and strength—a lot of strength, the strength of the common people who live, work, study, and play in peace.

CAMPO DA BOCCE: GENE AND SHIRLEY VILFORDI

UD Romers have embraced the timeless charm of Bocce, a friendly game dating back to 7000 BC. What is wonderful about this very Italian game is that it pulls down all the barriers between generations. Whether in their twenties or their eighties, whether grandchildren or grandparents—older people are usually extremely skilled!—players enjoy the opportunity to get together. Gene and Shirley, I am offering you the peach flower, representing good mood, sociability, and hope for a better future.

BUSINESS OFFICE: GIFT OF MARGIE & DAN CRUISE—IN HONOR OF MARGIE & BOYD BARKER

The Business Office, once a stable for animals, was completely renovated and is now a discreet and simple structure, its wooden ceilings adding a touch of rustic and rural elegance. I always say that the work of our office is hidden, not visible, but extremely important. Very close to the Business Office is a special plant called *Callistemon citrinus*, introduced to Europe from Australia at the Kew Gardens in London by Joseph Banks. This naturalist and botanist, a member of the Royal Society, accompanied James Cook during his first trip to Oceania in 1771. The *Callistemon* flower consists of massed stamens in the shape of a bottle brush. In Italy, they are called "*i pennacchi dei carabinieri*" (the carabinieri feathers); the national gendarmerie of Italy, in fact, wear special hats with distinctive upright plumes. Its brilliant red color looks fresh in late summer heat waves and warm in early winter. The word derives from ancient Greek *kalos*, for "beautiful," and *stemon*, for "stamen." A very appropriate name, underlining a beautiful inflorescence, though not its petals, which are absolutely invisible.

THE PERGOLA AND JAKE ADDISON

There is a place on campus that is always in my heart and thoughts and which is the last I am leaving with the reader. There is no sign on it, no plaque, making it more special than the others because everyone knows to whom that place is dedicated. I remember that when I first came to campus, my heart was immediately caught without even knowing why this place was so significant. Every now and then, I try to spend a few minutes sitting on its bench and just getting lost in my thoughts.

Just below the dorm, there is a romantic pergola—a small pavilion and sitting area decorated with cobblestones. This place is just a diamond among the other campus gemstones, and it was a gift to the campus in memory of Jake Addison by his UD Rome class.

OPPOSITE, TOP
The pergola. *Vasile Chiriac.*

OPPOSITE, BOTTOM
"Some say that unto bees is given a share of the Divine Intelligence and a draught of the springs of Heaven" (Virgil, *The Georgics*). *Vasile Chiriac.*

When I sit there, my thoughts come one after the other, just like the cycle of the four seasons. They come irrespective of my preferences, and they emerge when they think they are rightly due, one after the other. The whole pavilion is languorously covered with wisteria, a beautiful, elegant plant that hypnotizes with its charming lilac blossoms, while its draping vines distribute harmony and peace to those who sit under its shadow. Wisteria blossoms last only a short time, but the plant grows larger and larger throughout its life. It expands continuously, as if it were searching to acquire new wisdom and knowledge day after day, experience after experience. Like the UD Rome Program, the long vines of the plants are forever extending to seek new meanings and knowledge.

The plant stands as the perfect symbol of immortality and longevity; the vines' growth marks the generations passing, through which wisdom, patience, persistence, and endurance can be learned and practiced. The greatest things are difficult and take a long time but are always worth the effort. Hard times must always be endured in order to reach the beautiful ones.

INTERMEZZO. SUMMER ROME

ANDREW MORAN

Professors who have not taught at Due Santi sometimes assume that a stint in Rome is a paid vacation: two years of good food and wine, travel and leisure, on the university's dime. But Rome faculty will instead attest to how exhausting the semesters can be. On both campuses, the workload is heavy, but no one in Irving receives 105 papers or exams at a time nor has multiple appointments at various government offices to arrange for a *permesso di soggiorno*, nor is memorizing a two-hundred-page book in Italian in order to pass a driver's license exam. But for three months of the year, the stereotype of the Rome campus as a pastoral idyll *does* ring true: there are few pleasures like summer at Due Santi.

Like their colleagues back in Texas, Rome faculty turn to scholarship come May, and the staff remain busy with daily duties; running campus and preparing for the next semester are year-round tasks. But lunchtime may include a jog in the vineyard or a dip in the pool. And six o'clock often means, instead of a traffic jam on 183 or 114, enjoying Aperol spritzes on the terrace above the *mensa* or starting the fire for a dinner at the *forno*. Vacationing professors and assistants from past years always seem to be dropping by, and so one generation and another, with the help of a bottle of Due Santi Rosso, swap war stories into the night. Summer is a time to delight in the beauty of the campus and the company of its residents.

Yet even then some are at work from dawn until dark, in service to students ranging in age from fifteen to senior citizens. From its first summer, Due Santi has hosted a variety of programs. Dr. Wayne Ambler in 1994 started Shakespeare in Italy, and three years later, Dr. David Davies inaugurated Latin in Rome, academically demanding

but fun high school programs that in a quarter century have brought more than one thousand students to Rome, more than one hundred of whom later matriculated at UD. Shakespeare has since been directed by Drs. Theresa Kenney, Gregory Roper, and Andrew Moran, Latin by Drs. David Sweet and Karl Maurer. A third high school program, Rome and the Catholic Church, added in 2016, has been directed by Father James Oberle and Dr. Christopher Malloy. There have been various adult programs over the years, such as tours led by Professor Lyle Novinski, classes offered by the School of Ministry, and now the Braniff Graduate School's Classical Education in Rome. A friendly partnership with Ripon College in Wisconsin has brought its students and faculty to Due Santi since 2014. Most importantly, our own undergraduates unable to attend the fall or spring semesters have another opportunity to bloom in Rome. Since the inception of the summer option in 2012, Dr. Ron Rombs has labored tirelessly and created a Rome semester with its own distinct excellence that reflects his generosity and enthusiasm.

PREVIOUS
"Fill full your cups: feel no distress; / 'Tis only one great thought the less" (Hardy, "Drinking Song"). *Stephen Henderson.*

ABOVE
Shakespeare in Italy students at the *forno*, Summer 2013. *University of Dallas Advancement.*

AFTERWORD

THE GENIUS OF THE ROME PROGRAM

Gregory Roper

Most universities sponsor multiple study-abroad programs in multiple countries, tailored to students' interests; they take place most often during the junior year, after students have chosen and spent some time in their major. I confess that I have, especially back in my student days, felt occasional envy at this way of doing things. How fascinating would it have been to study on a program focused on a particular field—architecture or European finance or ecology—and have it happen later in my college career, when I was able to pick up on, and valuably engage with, those advanced topics. And to be able to choose from a smorgasbord of countries in which to study! A whole semester, or even year, in Ireland or Brazil or Botswana—the very thought filled this inveterate traveler with exotic dreams and fantasies. Yet now, older and more experienced and having taught for eight semesters on the UD Rome Program, I think that there is a particular and wonderful genius to the way we do it at UD, as well as a rich set of goods that those other programs do not have, that they cannot even reach, that are even occluded by those other ways of doing things.

I use *genius* here in an older sense understandable to those with UD's kind of education: a presiding or guardian spirit, a prevalent character, of a place or institution. When Christian Norberg-Schulz teaches about the *genius loci*, this is the meaning of the word he is using: the presiding spirit or character of a place that the architect must respect and work with, a kind of minor god hovering over the feel of the place. A Norberg-Schulz–trained architect would never think of putting a New Mexican pueblo-style house in the Virginia Blue Ridge Mountains, any more than he would design a Swiss

Jim Fougerousse, a man for all seasons. *Rome Campus Archives*.

A-frame for the Texas high prairie—neither would respect the spirit of the place. And with all due respect for Donald and Louie Cowan, who had the administrative vision and drive to make the program a reality, sustain it in its early years, and build it into its academic power, the presiding spirit of the UD Rome Program has always been a great bear of a minor god, Jim Fougerousse.

As is only proper, the origin story is melded of history and myth. It begins with Jim taking time off from UD to ride a motorcycle around Europe and then coming back to push his way into Don Cowan's office to suggest rather strongly that the university create a study-abroad program in Europe. One can only imagine Jim's well-over-six-foot frame in the president's doorway, his booming voice, his laughter and delight as he told of his Odyssean adventures and eventual *nostos* to Irving, which was then a lonely provincial Ithaka on the fringes of not just Dallas but, psychically, just about everywhere. The more factual part of the story—that Don and Louise Cowan went to a desalinization conference in Greece, caught the bug themselves, and found a convent in Rome to be the first home of the program—is the prose to go with this poetry.

So sing, then, O Muse, of the program they concocted, in that time half a century ago, a time that feels so distant and yet somehow so near at hand, partly because of what they did, what insights they brought to their thoughts, these three. Sing also of the goods they fashioned, in the program and more importantly in the students, through the decisions they made, the ways they chose not to blow with the prevailing winds.

Sing, also, of this genius—the man, the spirit—and of how his spirit still walks with students today, most of whom have never heard of him. Who was he, O Muse, and how can he still walk with them on Ten-Day, he who now, in Nestor's age, travels seldom from his home in Austria? My own memories let me add to many others, O Muse, as a way to begin.

When I went on my own Rome semester in the spring of 1982, Dr. Fougerousse and his family were with us at the Via del Pescaccio campus—already then a pretty run-down place, with heat for an hour or so a day, with the consequence that in February we'd have to warm our hands before class on the hot-water pipe that ran down the hallway outside of the only classroom. We had the superb Michael Waldstein to teach us Western Theo. Trad., overseeing so many of our spiritual transformations, and the ever-exuberant Fritz Wilhelmsen to teach us Philosophy of Man and challenge students in raucous, shouting chess matches, so we didn't lack for powerful figures. Yet even though he was not the director, and only taught us Lit. Trad. III in the hurried way it was done back then, we still knew some of the stories and still thought of Dr. Fougerousse as the source and energy of the Rome Program. He was a huge man with a huge voice and, most of all, a huge zest for life—even a little touched with this zest—and he taught us by example that we should have the same thirst for the experience of the semester. I thought of him as fundamentally fearless, someone who would try anything, lead us pretty much anywhere.

But he didn't want to lead us like little ducklings anywhere; he wanted us Romers to do it for ourselves. Dr. William Frank once told me that Jim had essentially a Christian Existentialist attitude toward the whole thing—academics, travel, Rome, Italy, Europe. "Jim's idea," Bill told me, "was to throw 'em in the deep end and let 'em figure out how to swim." The program reflected this, being much looser in those days. No hand-holding on-site lectures or tours; only one RA to shepherd more than one hundred students, and no attitude that he should solve our problems for us; and nothing in the way of organized entertainment. I shock students of today when I tell them that, except for a quick drive-by the first day in a Stoppini bus, I never made it to the Forum until nigh the last week of the semester, and without guides or professors to lecture to me, I had no idea what I was seeing. But it was this attitude, combined with the great love for the Western tradition Jim had imbibed at UD, that gave shape to the decisions of the program from the beginning and created the essential character it still keeps today, such that an alumnus from 1977, upon meeting a Spring Romer from 2017, can share almost identical academic and personal experiences.

First—and here I cannot help but think that a young Jim Fougerousse may have had some influence on Don and Louise Cowan—they had the inspiration to send students over in their sophomore year. This is quite distinct from what almost every other study-abroad program does. Other programs tend to wait until the junior year, once students are established in their majors and more mature. But UD sends students over quite early, when they are still in formation. Not freshman year, mind you, for we need to introduce them to, start them on thinking, what a UD education is all about. They need to encounter Homer, the *Republic*, Under the Bible, the *Nicomachean Ethics* and Dante and Milton; they need to be inspired with the heroic, taught that their souls are like a city, and brought to encounter Virtue as a Habit; and they need to travel through hell, examining the darker side of the human (and of themselves), climb laboriously up through Purgatory, re-training themselves to love properly, and soar through heaven. They need Ecclesiastes's astringency and Isaiah's soaring poetry, Paul's theological vision and the power of the Gospels. But at that point, they are still young, fired with ideas and ideals, still figuring themselves out. Most Romers, Fall and Spring, still are not quite sure who they are; majors are still somewhat in flux, and they are discovering their interests, talents, and loves (human, intellectual, and moral). Don and Louise Cowan had the insight that this is the perfect time to send them abroad and to send them to Rome, a place that simultaneously unsettles and centers the nineteen-year-old romantic. Rome, and Roman culture, is so different from modern suburban America—especially in the early years, when it was only a few steps above the teeming bustle of a third-world country—that it constantly challenges the not-so-long-ago-freshman to perceive things differently, to try different ways of being, before opinions and self-conceptions get too settled. Sophomores, I've found, are some of my favorite students: past the bungling craziness (or sheltered timidity) of freshmen, not anywhere near the exhausted knowing seniors, they are wide-eyed, still innocent enough and yet mature and prepared enough to absorb the power of their experiences, willing to try things, ready to be changed by the experience. I seem to spy Jim's intrepid spirit inspiring this decision.

Second, UD had the great sense to bring over the *entire* sophomore group (or as much of it as possible) as one big rollicking festival gathering. On the UD Rome Program, students of different majors, avocations, and backgrounds mix promiscuously. A Lit. Trad. III class has biologists and chemists as well as English majors and historians; politics majors offer their opinions in Western Civilization I alongside painters and potters; and economics majors must discuss Augustine's *Confessions* alongside philosophy majors and physicists. And it's not just in class. The campus is so small that one cannot help but rub shoulders with others in the everyday: in the *mensa*, on a bus in Greece, in the campus chapel, the Rome class comes together to share interests, fascinations, experiences, and questions. One of Jim Fougerousse's great loves is the grand conversation with his family and friends, spread around a table, the drink and food spurring on great talk of life and its meaning among the quotidian details of the day. Don and Louise, as southerners, shared this idea of the best life as an endless *symposium*. And so they constructed a study-abroad program to offer as many opportunities as possible for this to happen. Unlike most study-abroad programs, which fragment the student body into narrower and narrower fields of specialization and have the students return to campus even more estranged from their fellow students than their multiversity had already made them, both intellectually and culturally, UD Rome is an enormous tool to fight against the trend toward the multiversity; it more than anything else helps the students experience a *uni*versity. I loved the moments when the physics major (who missed her math classes so much she'd google calculus problems in her free time) would step up and debate the theology of *King Lear*, and I had the best final exam of my life when a math major wrote that tragedy could best be explained by chaos theory. And may I say, this carries over for many years; a UD senior can meet an alum from thirty years before, of any major, and share, as if yesterday, similar experiences from those magical three months and the growth they experienced.

Of course, all of this centers on the genius of choosing Rome and the core as the subject to be studied there. Here, without any historical justification whatsoever, I imagine Jim, with his love of all things German and Austrian, battling with Louise and Don about the location of the program. I can imagine him holding out for Salzburg or Vienna or Fribourg; here he gives way to the Cowans' higher vision. For Louise knew that the great question of Western culture is "What does Athens have to do with Jerusalem?" and that Rome embodies the answer. And here, of course, all three of these cede their role as genius of the program to Peter and Paul, Benedict and Francis, Bonaventure and Aquinas.

Once again the contrast and wise vision could not be clearer. In other programs, students tend to study the culture, the politics, the art and architecture, of the place being visited; that is the *raison d'etre* of such a program. You might go to Brussels to study the contemporary world of the EU or Costa Rica to study environmental change in the rainforest. You learn, usually, from professors from the native country and experience their differing attitudes and points of view. The purpose of those programs is ec-centric, to get the students away from the center of their lives and cultures, to give them something outside, new and different. UD students fully experience Rome and Italy as different places, of course, but the Rome Program asks students to lift their eyes to something larger and more comprehensive: the concept of Rome as the central place, actual and conceptual, of Western civilization. And in that sense, the genius of employing UD professors, teaching the UD core, is to be *centric*, not eccentric, to be centripetal, not centrifugal.

On the Greece trip, the program travels together as a class. We move into the heart of the curriculum, the heart of Western civilization. Students arrive together at the Pnyx, the Areopagus, the Parthenon—that triptych of democracy, law, and faith that is what Western civilization is all about—and they even travel together all the way back to the first day of Lit. Trad. I, up the ramp, through the Lion Gate, to the citadel of Agamemnon, to the misty origins of Mycenean culture (and then, on their way to lunch, past the Kleitemnestra Hotel, offering "bed and bath"; its owners apparently do not expect any of the tourists to have read Aeschylus). Students and professors and their children see these together, finding the core of who we are in the West as a unified group. There's a reason students call the five courses in Rome "the core of the core" and experience their Rome semester that way; at no other time are the connections between physical place, the Western intellectual tradition, the Catholic intellectual tradition, the contemporary and the ancient, the intellectual and the spiritual, made more powerfully manifest. As a result, they can return to their own culture and, to misquote T.S. Eliot only slightly, end where they began, see it again for the first time, and appreciate America's—and their own—place in the larger sea that is Western culture.

Finally, there has always been a peculiar genius of the Ten-Day break and its contrast with the Greece trip. Here again, Jim Fougerousse seems to occupy his throne as a minor god, for just a few weeks after that communal experience of Greece, we boot them off campus for ten days. And here, as any Romer will tell you, is when the really interesting stories take place: odd encounters with natives, ugly American tourists, and hilarious Aussies; hopeless footraces to catch trains already pulling out of the station; and weird coincidences. Students once told me of waking up in the middle of Poland in the middle of the night to find their train car had separated from the main track; it was sitting on a siding, empty except for four puzzled Romers and a few highly armed Polish soldiers who spoke no English. Another told me of waking on the floor of a train in eastern Europe, where she had very comfortably spent the night in her sleeping bag; now, to her surprise, the sleeping bag had been neatly sliced from head to toe and the expensive camera next to her had been quietly lifted. (The terror of what else could have happened—and the gratitude to Providence that it did not—only set in later, she said; this, too, is common to Romers.) The genre of the Ten-Day story is rich with such incidents and varied as the possibilities of youthful naïveté, overconfidence—not to say utter cluelessness—and the exigencies of other cultures can make them, giving rise to the phrase that predates my own Spring 1982 Rome experience: "God looks after fools and UD students." I learned that phrase my freshman year and once in Rome quickly learned (and experienced) how true it was. A few weeks later, I learned its corollary: "And most of the time, not even He can tell the difference."

Because of lawyers and cultural changes, we have to be a little more organized, a little more protective, a little more careful and helpful now, over the course of the semester. And the internet allows students to stay closer to home than ever before: an hour after their arrival in August, students are checking the latest baseball scores and Facebooking with family and friends. (In 1982, I called home exactly twice the entire semester; the one-second delay was so irritating that my parents and I mutually agreed to give up and just write letters.) But the Ten-Day experience still allows that *frisson* of freedom, responsibility, and risk that allows students to grow up without parents, professors, RAs, or administrators taking care of them.

The genius of Ten-Day is that we loose them on a continent, with only their backpacks, their money, their wits, their upbringing, and their education to help them. And we tell them they can't come back, even after nine days. In today's world of safe spaces, overscheduled kids, and helicopter parents, UD still puts Jim's vision at the center; it still has the presence of mind to push them out of the nest. And it works: they come back, unbathed, tired, and a little scruffy but with their chests puffed out. If you can handle losing your way deep in Scotland's Highlands or helping a sick roommate find a doctor's office in a tawdry room behind a Budapest bar on a Saturday night, you can handle anything.

Jim Fougerousse at the beginning, with Sister Georgianne Segner, SSND. *Rome Campus Archives.*

I always told the students to beware Day Seven, for by that point they have been gone a good while, are tired, hungry, and nearing the end of their funds, but it is still a few days before they are allowed back on campus. For a few years, the Day Seven story became a Rome subgenre. The early riser in my family, I was on the terrazzo above the *mensa* early one Sunday morning when I heard the gate open and close; I hadn't forgotten that it was the last day of the break and the students would start straggling in, but this was pretty early—usually they didn't make it back until late afternoon or evening.

I heard them before I could see them.

"Roper! Where is Dr. Roper! We need Dr. Roper!" A group of four male students—backpacks on, disheveled, dirty—walked down the road to the campus center shouting up, without realizing it, to exactly where I was standing. I leaned over the terrazzo and showed myself, hissing in a stage whisper, "What is the matter with you idiots? I have sleeping kids in my apartment!"

"You cursed us!" they said.

"I did nothing of the sort," I said indignantly. What was this about?

"No, you cursed us. You have to hear our Day Seven story."

"All right. Come up here. If you'll quiet down, I'll make a pot of coffee and you can tell me all about it."

I don't remember the story at all, probably because it was just like all the others. But what I do remember is this: as they shook their heads, telling me one more bizarre narrative laced with understandable missteps, communication problems, foolish decisions, and just dumb luck—which is, of course, Providence—they were laughing.

And did they ever suck down our coffee.

Dr. John Alvis, who taught me Homer and Dante, once said that there are only two questions of a truly liberal education: What is the nature of reality and how should a life be lived? By taking the students at the precise point when those questions have become insistent—when they have been primed for the questions but have few if any answers; by taking them into the heart of their culture, their faith, their education; by putting before them professors and texts to drive them ever deeper into the two questions; by letting them stand on the earth where those questions were addressed by drama, art, architecture, philosophy, and a Church; by then turning them loose to figure it out in the midst of that richness, the Rome Program teaches students what it means, as Rilke said, to live the questions. It points them toward shaping intelligent, wise, heartfelt answers that can shape their lives. When you see the transformation of these students over those three months, you know that a genius was at work and still is.

APPENDIX

UNIVERSITY OF DALLAS ROME PROGRAM CAMPUSES, FACULTY, AND STAFF

CAMPUS LOCATIONS, 1970–2020

September 1970–December 1971
Casa Generalizia, SSND
Via della Stazione Aurelia, 95
00165 Roma, Italia

January 1972–May 1973
International Center
Via della Pisana, 1301
00163 Roma, Italia

May 1973–May 1989
Hotel La Villa
Via Del Pescaccio, 103
00166 Roma, Italia

August 1989–December 1992
Villa S. Cecilia
Via Argelato, 56
00127 Vitinia, Roma, Italia

January 1993–May 1994
Hotel degli Etruschi
Via Roma, 101
00066 Manziana, Roma, Italia

June 1994–present
The Eugene Constantin Campus, Due Santi
Via Dei Ceraseti, 12
00040 Frattochie, Roma, Italia

FACULTY AND STAFF, 1970–2020

Fall 1970

Father Damian Fandal, OP, Director, Chaplain, Theology, Philosophy
John Alvis, English, Politics
Kathy Alvis, History
Robert Forlitti, Italian
Manus Isensee, Assistant
Sybil Novinski, Coordinator of the Rome Program

Spring 1971

Father Thomas Cain, OP, Director, Theology, Philosophy, Chaplain
John Alvis, History, Politics
Kathy Alvis, History
Christine Ciembronowicz, English, Assistant
Sister M. Augusta Perkin, Italian
Manus Isensee, Assistant
Sybil Novinski, Coordinator of the Rome Program

Fall 1971

Father Thomas Cain, OP, Director, Theology, Philosophy, Chaplain
Christine Ciembronowicz, English
Helen de Alvarez, Philosophy
Leo Paul de Alvarez, History, Politics
Tom Jenner, Philosophy
Sister M. Augusta Perkin, Italian
Sybil Novinski, Coordinator of the Rome Program

Spring 1972

Father Thomas Cain, Director, Philosophy, Chaplain
Father David Balás, O. Cist., Theology
Chris Ciembronowicz, English, Assistant
Helen de Alvarez, Philosophy
Leo Paul de Alvarez, History, Politics
Jim Scully, Assistant
Sybil Novinski, Coordinator of the Rome Program

Fall 1972

Father Thomas Cain, OP, Director, Theology, Philosophy, Chaplain
E.C. Curtsinger, English, History
Jane Fitzgibbons, Politics
Lina Milozza, Italian
Jim Scully, Philosophy
Sybil Novinski, Coordinator of the Rome Program

Spring 1973

Father Thomas Cain, OP, Director, Theology, Philosophy, Chaplain
E.C. Curtsinger, English, History
Jane Fitzgibbons, Politics, Assistant
Lina Milozza, Italian
Jim Scully, Philosophy, Dean
Sybil Novinski, Coordinator of the Rome Program

Fall 1973

David Brown, Director, History
Mike Bordelon, Politics
Jane Gibson Brown, English
Father Norman Fenton, OP, Philosophy, Theology, Chaplain
Mary Bordelon, Secretary
Lucas Godinez, Assistant

Spring 1974

David Brown, Director, History
Mike Bordelon, Politics
Jane Gibson Brown, English
Father Norman Fenton, OP, Philosophy, Theology, Chaplain
Mary Bordelon, Secretary
Lucas Godinez, Assistant

Fall 1974

David Brown, Director, History
Jane Brown, English
Father Norman Fenton, OP, Philosophy, Chaplain
Father Charles Fiore, Theology
Ginny Lombardo, Politics
Signorina Prestia, Italian
Father Robert Butler, Assistant Chaplain
Thomas Stone, Assistant

Spring 1975

David Brown, Director, History
Jane Brown, English
Father Norman Fenton, OP, Philosophy, Chaplain
Ginny Lombardo, Politics
Signorina Prestia, Italian
Thomas Stone, Assistant

Fall 1975

Robert Scott Dupree, Director, English, Italian
Father David Balás, O. Cist., Theology
Father Gilbert Hardy, O. Cist., Philosophy, Chaplain
Christopher Manion, History, Politics
Susan Dupree, Secretary
Mike Treadway, Assistant

Spring 1976

Robert Scott Dupree, Director, English, Italian
Father David Balás, O. Cist., Theology
Father Gilbert Hardy, O. Cist., Philosophy, Chaplain
Christopher Manion, History, Politics
Susan Dupree, Secretary
Mike Treadway, Assistant
Denise Michalka, Rome Office Coordinator

Fall 1976

Robert Scott Dupree, Director, History, Art
David Balás, O. Cist., Theology
Father Damian Fandal, OP, Philosophy, Chaplain
Father Russo, Italian
Dennis Slattery, English
Susan Dupree, Secretary
Bill McCalpin, Assistant
Denise Michalka, Rome Office Coordinator

Spring 1977

Robert Scott Dupree, Director, History, Art
David Balás, O. Cist., Theology
Rosanna Hoefer, Italian
Father Benedict Monostori, O. Cist., Philosophy, Chaplain
Dennis Slattery, English
Susan Dupree, Secretary
Bill McCalpin, Assistant
Denise Michalka, Rome Office Coordinator

Fall 1977

Dennis Slattery, Director, English
Father Richard Butler, OP, Philosophy
Father Robert Hennessy, OP, Theology
Rosanna Hoefer, Italian
Father Andrew Miehls, OP, History, Art, Chaplain
David Baum, Assistant
Sandy Slattery, Secretary
Denise Michalka, Rome Office Coordinator

Spring 1978

Dennis Slattery, Director, English
Rosanna Hoefer, Italian
William Lydecker, Art
Ron Muller, Philosophy
Father Cho Dinh Phan, Theology, Philosophy, Chaplain
Joe Stiles, History
David Baum, Assistant
Sandy Slattery, Secretary
Denise Michalka, Rome Office Coordinator

Fall 1978

Ron Muller, Director, Philosophy
Eileen Gregory, English
Rosanna Hoefer, Italian
Father James Lehrberger, O. Cist., Theology, Philosophy, Chaplain
Christian Norberg-Schulz, Art History
Lyle Novinski, Art History
Joe Stiles, History
Pat Daly, Assistant
Lucy Muller, Assistant
Julie Slavik, Assistant
Steve Slavik, Assistant
Denise Michalka, Rome Office Coordinator

Spring 1979

Ron Muller, Director, Philosophy
Eileen Gregory, English
Rosanna Hoefer, Italian
Father James Lehrberger, O, Cist., Theology, Philosophy, Chaplain
Christian Norberg-Schulz, Art History
Lyle Novinski, Art History
Joe Stiles, History
Pat Daly, Assistant
Lucy Muller, Assistant
Julie Slavik, Assistant
Steve Slavik, Assistant
Denise Michalka, Rome Office Coordinator

Fall 1979

E.C. Curtsinger, Director, English
Rosanna Hoefer, Italian
Father James Lehrberger, O. Cist., Theology, Chaplain
Christian Norberg-Schulz, Art History
Lyle Novinski, Art History
Dan Utrecht, Philosophy
Alexandra Wilhelmsen, History
Barbara Curtsinger, Assistant
Pat Daly, Assistant
John Goeller, Assistant
Dave Wright, Assistant
Debbie Wright, Assistant
Denise Michalka, Rome Office Coordinator

Spring 1980

E.C. Curtsinger, Director, English
John Crosby, Philosophy
Rosanna Hoefer, Italian
Father James Lehrberger, O. Cist., Theology, Chaplain
Christian Norberg-Schulz, Art History
Lyle Novinski, Art History
Joe Stiles, History
Barbara Curtsinger, Assistant
Pat Daly, Assistant
John Goeller, Assistant
Dave Wright, Assistant
Debbie Wright, Assistant
Denise Michalka, Rome Office Coordinator

Fall 1980

E.C. Curtsinger, Director, English
Rosanna Hoefer, Italian
Father James Lehrberger, O. Cist, Theology, Chaplain, Philosophy
Rachel McClung, Art Assistant
Ron Muller, Philosophy
James Petzel, History
Anna Marie Norberg-Schulz, Italian
Christian Norberg-Schulz, Art History
Lyle Novinski, Art History
Barbara Curtsinger, Assistant
Mike Curtsinger, Assistant
Shelley Curtsinger, Assistant
Jake Gallerano, Assistant
Denise Schuler, Rome Office Coordinator

Spring 1981

E.C. Curtsinger, Director, English
Rosanna Hoefer, Italian
Father James Lehrberger, O. Cist., Theology, Chaplain, Philosophy
Rachel McClung, Art Assistant
Ron Muller, Phil of Being
James Petzel, History
Anna Marie Norberg-Schulz, Italian
Christian Norberg-Schulz, Art History
Lyle Novinski, Art History
Barbara Curtsinger, Assistant
Mike Curtsinger, Assistant
Shelley Curtsinger, Assistant
Jake Gallerano, Assistant
Denise Schuler, Rome Office Coordinator

Fall 1981

Roy T. Jacob Jr., Director, Math
James Fougerousse, English
Anna Marie Norberg-Schulz, Italian
Christian Norberg-Schulz, Art History
Lyle Novinski, Art History
James Petzel, History
Michael Waldstein, Theology, Greek, Latin
Robert Wood, Philosophy
Father Nelson, Chaplain
Dan Harkins, Assistant
Peggy Harkins, Assistant
Denise Schuler, Rome Office Coordinator

Spring 1982

Roy T. Jacob Jr., Director, Math
James Fougerousse, English
Anna Marie Norberg-Schulz, Italian
Christian Norberg-Schulz, Art History
Lyle Novinski, Art History
James Petzel, History
Michael Waldstein, Theology, Greek, Latin
Frederick Wilhelmsen, Philosophy
Dan Harkins, Assistant
Peggy Harkins, Assistant
Denise Schuler, Rome Office Coordinator

Fall 1982

Roy T. Jacob Jr., Director, Math
Father Thomas Carroll, Chaplain, Theology
James Fougerousse, English
Anna Marie Norberg-Schulz, Italian
Christian Norberg-Schulz, Art History
Lyle Novinski, Art History
James Petzel, History
Michael Waldstein, Theology, Greek, Latin
Frederick Wilhelmsen, Philosophy
Dan Harkins, Assistant
Peggy Harkins, Assistant
Denise Schuler, Rome Office Coordinator

Spring 1983

Roy T. Jacob Jr., Director, Math
James Fougerousse, Acting Director, English
Father Thomas Carroll, Chaplain, Theology
John Crosby, Philosophy
Anna Marie Norberg-Schulz, Italian
Christian Norberg-Schulz, Art History
Lyle Novinski, Art History
James Petzel, History
Michael Waldstein, Theology, Greek, Latin
Dan Harkins, Assistant
Peggy Harkins, Assistant
Denise Schuler, Rome Office Coordinator

Fall 1983

James Fougerousse, Director, English
Father Thomas Carroll, Chaplain, Theology
Father Gilbert Hardy, O. Cist., Philosophy
Anna Marie Norberg-Schulz, Italian
Christian Norberg-Schulz, Art History
Lyle Novinski, Art History
Kathleen Wellman, History
Dan Harkins, Associate Director
Peggy Harkins, Assistant Director
Denise Schuler, Rome Office Coordinator

Spring 1984

James Fougerousse, Director, English
Father Thomas Carroll, Chaplain, Theology
Naomi Lusi, Italian
Anna Marie Norberg-Schulz, Italian
Christian Norberg-Schulz, Art History
Lyle Novinski, Art History
Dennis Sepper, Philosophy
Kathleen Wellman, History
Dan Harkins, Associate Director
Peggy Harkins, Assistant Director
Jeff Patterson, Assistant Director
Denise Schuler, Rome Office Coordinator

Fall 1984

James Fougerousse, Director, English
Father Thomas Carroll, Chaplain, Theology
Naomi Lusi, Italian
Anna Marie Norberg-Schulz, Italian
Christian Norberg-Schulz, Art History
Lyle Novinski, Art History
Dennis Sepper, Philosophy
Kathleen Wellman, History
Jeff Patterson, Associate Director
Annette Patterson, Assistant to the Director
Denise Schuler, Rome Office Coordinator

Spring 1985

James Fougerousse, Director, German, English
Anna Marie Norberg-Schulz, Italian
Christian Norberg-Schulz, Art History
Dennis Sepper, Philosophy
Charlotte Sullivan, Art History
David Sweet, Classics, English
Kathleen Wellman, History
Jeff Patterson, Associate Director
Annette Patterson, Assistant to Director
Greg Wood, Assistant to Director
Denise Schuler, Rome Office Coordinator

Fall 1985

James Fougerousse, Director, German, English
Father Thomas Carroll, Chaplain, Theology
George McClure, History
Anna Marie Norberg-Schulz, Italian
Christian Norberg-Schulz, Art History
Charlotte Sullivan, Art History
Frederick Wilhelmsen, Philosophy
Chris Kuehler, Assistant to Director
Denise Schuler, Rome Office Coordinator

Spring 1986

James Fougerousse, Director, German, English
Father Thomas Carroll, Chaplain, Theology
George McClure, History
Anna Marie Norberg-Schulz, Italian
Christian Norberg-Schulz, Art History
Charlotte Sullivan, Art History
Frederick Wilhelmsen, Philosophy
Father George Schemberi, Associate Director
Chris Kuehler, Assistant to Director
Denise Schuler, Rome Office Coordinator

Fall 1986

James Fougerousse, Director
Regis Martin, Theology
Anna Marie Norberg-Schulz, Italian
Christian Norberg-Schulz, Art, History
Lyle Novinski, Greece
Katherine Sorensen, English
Charlotte Sullivan, Art History
Frederick Wilhelmsen, Philosophy
Michael Wolfe, History
Randy Irlbeck, Assistant
Denise Schuler, Rome Office Coordinator

Spring 1987

James Fougerousse, Director
Regis Martin, Theology
Anna Marie Norberg-Schulz, Italian
Christian Norberg-Schulz, Art, History
Lyle Novinski, Greece
Katherine Sorensen, English
Charlotte Sullivan, Art History
Frederick Wilhelmsen, Philosophy
Michael Wolfe, History
Father George Schemberi, Associate Director
Randy Irlbeck, Assistant
Denise Schuler, Rome Office Coordinator

Fall 1987

James Fougerousse, Director, English
Father Gilbert Hardy, O. Cist., Philosophy, Chaplain
Regis Martin, Theology
Anna Marie Norberg-Schulz, Italian
Christian Norberg-Schulz, Art, History
Lyle Novinski, Greece
Charlotte Sullivan, Art History
Brian Whalen, Assistant Director, English
Michael Wolfe, History
Randy Irlbeck, Associate Director
Denise Schuler, Rome Office Coordinator

Spring 1988

James Fougerousse, Director, English
Father Gilbert Hardy, O. Cist, Philosophy, Chaplain
Regis Martin, Theology
Anna Marie Norberg-Schulz, Italian
Christian Norberg-Schulz, Art, History
Lyle Novinski, Greece
Charlotte Sullivan, Art History
Brian Whalen, Assistant Director, English
Michael Wolfe, History
Randy Irlbeck, Associate Director
Denise Schuler, Rome Office Coordinator

Fall 1988

James Fougerousse, Director, English
Wayne Ambler, History, Politics
Jose Garbriel Cortes, Theology
William Frank, Philosophy
Anna Marie Norberg-Schulz, Italian
Christian Norberg-Schulz, Art, History
Lyle Novinski, Greece
Charlotte Sullivan, Art History
Brian Whalen, Associate Director, English
Randy Irlbeck, Associate Director
Father Patrick Desmond, LC, Chaplain
Father Vincent McMahon, LC, Chaplain
Annmarie Whalen, Asst. Director
Denise Schuler, Rome Office Coordinator

Spring 1989

Brian Whalen, Director
Wayne Ambler, History, Politics
Jose Gabriel Cortes, Theology
Eugene Curtsinger, English
William Frank, Philosophy
Christian Norberg-Schulz, Art History
Lyle Novinski, Greece
Charlotte Sullivan, Art and Architecture
Randy Irlbeck, Associate Director
Annmarie Whalen, Assistant Director
Father Patrick Desmond, LC, Chaplain
Corlin Ambler, English Assistant
Therese Frank, English Assistant
Denise Schuler, Rome Office Coordinator

Fall 1989

Brian Whalen, Director
Wayne Ambler, Politics, History
Sister Saint John Begnaud, SSMN, English
Christopher Colvin, Philosophy
Father Paul Lockey, Theology, Chaplain
Anna Maria Norberg-Schulz, Italian
Christian Norberg-Schulz, Art History
Lyle Novinski, Greece
Charlotte Sullivan, Art History
Andrew Favorite, Assistant
Tony Thompson, Assistant
Denise Schuler, Rome Office Coordinator

Spring 1990

Brian Whalen, Director
Wayne Ambler, Politics, History
Sister Saint John Begnaud, SSMN, English
Christopher Colvin, Philosophy
Father Paul Lockey, Theology, Chaplain
Anna Maria Norberg-Schulz, Italian
Christian Norberg-Schulz, Art History
Lyle Novinski, Greece
Charlotte Sullivan, Art History
Andrew Favorite, Assistant
Tony Thompson, Assistant
Denise Schuler, Rome Office Coordinator
Randy Irlbeck, Acting Rome Coordinator

Fall 1990

Brian Whalen, Director
Christopher Colvin, Philosophy
Father Paul Lockey, Associate Director, Chaplain, Theology
Bruce MacQueen, English
Anna Maria Norberg-Schulz, Italian
Christian Norberg-Schulz, Art History
Lyle Novinski, Greece
Charles Sullivan, History
Charlotte Sullivan, Art History
Richard Ellis, Assistant
Anthony Thompson, Assistant
Denise Schuler, Rome Office Coordinator
Randy Irlbeck, Acting Rome Office Coordinator

Spring 1991

Brian Whalen, Director
Christopher Colvin, Philosophy
Father Paul Lockey, Associate Director, Chaplain, Theology
Bruce MacQueen, English
Anna Maria Norberg-Schulz, Italian
Christian Norberg-Schulz, Art History
Lyle Novinski, Greece
Charles Sullivan, History
Charlotte Sullivan, Art History
Richard Ellis, Assistant
Anthony Thompson, Assistant
Denise Schuler, Rome Office Coordinator

Fall 1991

Father Gilbert Hardy, O. Cist., Director, Theology
Father Robert Maguire, O. Cist., English, Chaplain
Anna Maria Norberg-Schulz, Italian
Christian Norberg-Schulz, Art History
Lyle Novinski, Greece
Dennis Sepper, Philosophy
Charlotte Sullivan, Art History
Kathleen Wellman, History
Hayden Head, Assistant
Sue Head, Assistant
Jeff Mobus, Assistant
Lisa Mobus, Assistant
Randy Irlbeck, Dui Santi Construction Coordinator
Denise Schuler, Rome Program Coordinator

Spring 1992

Father Gilbert Hardy, O. Cist., Director, Theology
Father Robert Maguire, O. Cist., English, Chaplain
Anna Maria Norberg-Schulz, Italian
Christian Norberg-Schulz, Art History
Lyle Novinski, Greece
Dennis Sepper, Philosophy
Charlotte Sullivan, Art History
Kathleen Wellman, History
Hayden Head, Assistant
Sue Head, Assistant
Jeff Mobus, Assistant
Lisa Mobus, Assistant
Randy Irlbeck, Dui Santi Construction Coordinator
Denise Schuler, Rome Program Coordinator

Fall 1992

Father Gilbert Hardy, O. Cist., Director
Anita Guerra, Human Figure
Lisa Mobus, Italian
Christian Norberg-Schulz, Art History
John Norris, Theology
Janet Smith, Philosophy
Charlotte Sullivan, Art History
David Sweet, English
Paul Ziegler, History
Jeff Mobus, Business Manager
Mike Craigue, Assistant
Alison Gower Assistant
Sybil C. Novinski, Assistant
Randy Irlbeck, Due Santi Construction Coordinator
Sue Head, Rome Office Coordinator

Spring 1993

Pat Daly, Director
Lisa Mobus, Italian
Christian Norberg-Schulz, Art History
John Norris, Theology
Janet Smith, Philosophy
Charlotte Sullivan, Art History
David Sweet, English
Paul Ziegler, History
Jeff Mobus, Business Manager
Mike Craigue, Assistant
Alison Gower Assistant
Sybil C. Novinski, Assistant
Randy Irlbeck, Due Santi Construction Coordinator
Sue Head, Rome Office Coordinator

Fall 1993

John Norris, Director, Theology
Lisa Mobus, Italian
Christian Norberg-Schulz, Art History
James Oehling, History
Janet Smith, Philosophy
Charlotte Sullivan, Art History
David Sweet, English
Jeff Mobus, Business Manager
Matt Clark, Assistant
Alison Gower, Assistant
Sybil C. Novinski, Assistant
Randy Irlbeck, Due Santi Construction Coordinator
Sue Head, Rome Office Coordinator

Spring 1994

John Norris, Director, Theology
Lisa Mobus, Italian
Christian Norberg-Schulz, Art History
James Oehling, History
Janet Smith, Philosophy
Charlotte Sullivan, Art History
David Sweet, English
Jeff Mobus, Business Manager
Matt Clark, Assistant
Alison Gower, Assistant
Sybil C. Novinski, Assistant
Randy Irlbeck, Due Santi Construction Coordinator
Sue Head, Rome Office Coordinator

Fall 1994

John Norris, Academic Director, Theology
Randy Irlbeck, Campus Director
Wayne Ambler, History
David Davies, English
Anita Guerra, Human Figure
Father James Lehrberger, O. Cist., Philosophy, Chaplain
Lisa Mobus, Italian
Charlotte Sullivan, Art History
Jeff Mobus, Business Manager
Matt Clark, Assistant
Lisa Pelletier, Assistant
Sue Head, Rome Office Coordinator

Spring 1995

John Norris, Academic Director, Theology
Randy Irlbeck, Campus Director
Wayne Ambler, History
David Davies, English
Anita Guerra, Human Figure
Father James Lehrberger, O. Cist., Philosophy, Chaplain
Lisa Mobus, Italian
Charlotte Sullivan, Art History
Jeff Mobus, Business Manager
Matt Clark, Assistant
Lisa Pelletier, Assistant

Fall 1995

Wayne Ambler, Academic Director, History
Randy Irlbeck, Campus Director
David Davies, English
Mark Goodwin, Theology
Lisa Mobus, Italian
Patrick Powers, Philosophy
Charlotte Sullivan, Art History
Monsignor Nevin Klinger, Chaplain
Jeff Mobus, Business Manager
Travis Curtright, Assistant
Lisa Pelletier, Assistant
Sybil Novinski, Rome Office Coordinator

Spring 1996

Wayne Ambler, Academic Director, History
Randy Irlbeck, Campus Director
David Davies, English
Mark Goodwin, Theology
Philip Larrey, Philosophy
Lisa Mobus, Italian
Araf Ali Nayed, Philosophy
Charlotte Sullivan, Art History
Monsignor Nevin Klinger, Chaplain
Jeff Mobus, Business Manager
Travis Curtright, Assistant
Lisa Pelletier, Assistant

Fall 1996

Wayne Ambler, Academic Director, History
Randy Irlbeck, Campus Director
Therese Frank, Theology
William Frank, Philosophy
Anita Guerra, Human Figure
Theresa Kenney, English
Lisa Mobus, Italian
Christian Norberg-Schulz, Art History
Charlotte Sullivan, Art History
Monsignor Nevin Klinger, Chaplain
Jeff Mobus, Business Manager
Travis Curtright, Assistant
Catherine Horan, Assistant
Sybil Novinski Sutton, Rome Office Coordinator

Spring 1997

Wayne Ambler, Academic Director, History
Randy Irlbeck, Campus Director
Therese Frank, Theology
William Frank, Philosophy
Lisa Mobus, Italian
Christian Norberg-Schulz, Art History
Charlotte Sullivan, Art History
Gerard Wegemer, English
Monsignor Nevin Klinger, Chaplain
Jeff Mobus, Business Manager
Travis Curtright, Assistant
Catherine Horan, Assistant
Sybil Novinski Sutton, Rome Office Coordinator

Fall 1997

Wayne Ambler, Program Director, History
Randy Irlbeck, Campus Director
Therese Frank, Theology
William Frank, Philosophy
Anita Guerra, Human Figure
Lisa Mobus, Italian
Christian Norberg-Schulz, Art History
Charlotte Sullivan, Art History
Sarah Thurow, English
Father James Conley, Chaplain
Jeff Mobus, Business Manager
Sarah Dawson, Assistant
Dustin Gish, Assistant
Joe Weinpel, Assistant
Sybil Novinski Sutton, Rome Office Coordinator

Spring 1998

Wayne Ambler, Program Director, History
Randy Irlbeck, Campus Director
Laura Flusche, Art History
Therese Frank, Theology
William Frank, Philosophy
Eileen Gregory, English
Lisa Mobus, Italian
Christian Norberg-Schulz, Art History
Charlotte Sullivan, Art History
Father James Conley, Chaplain
Jeff Mobus, Business Manager
Sarah Dawson, Assistant
Dustin Gish, Assistant
Joe Weinpel, Assistant
Sybil Novinski Sutton, Rome Office Coordinator

Fall 1998

Wayne Ambler, Program Director, History
Randy Irlbeck, Campus Director
Scott Crider, English
Laura Flusche, Art History
Therese Frank, Theology
William Frank, Philosophy
Lisa Mobus, Italian
Christian Norberg-Schulz, Art History
Charlotte Sullivan, Art History
Father James Conley, Chaplain
Jeff Mobus, Business Manager
Sarah Dawson, Assistant
Dustin Gish, Assistant
Joe Weinpel, Assistant
Sybil Novinski Sutton, Rome Office Coordinator

Spring 1999

William Frank, Program Director, Philosophy
Randy Irlbeck, Campus Director
Scott Crider, English
Laura Flusche, Art History
Therese Frank, Theology
Lisa Mobus, Italian
Christian Norberg-Schulz, Art History
Charlotte Sullivan, Art History
Sarah Thurow, History
Father James Conley, Chaplain
Jeff Mobus, Business Manager
Sarah Dawson, Assistant
Dustin Gish, Assistant
Joe Weinpel, Assistant
Sybil Novinski Sutton, Rome Office Coordinator

Fall 1999

Wayne Ambler, Program Director
Randy Irlbeck, Campus Director
Scott Crider, English
Laura Flusche, Art History
Peter Hatlie, History
Michael McShane, Philosophy
Lisa Mobus, Italian
Michael Terranova, Theology
Father James Conley, Chaplain
Jeff Mobus, Campus Manager
Sarah Dawson, Assistant
Dustin Gish, Assistant
Joe Weinpel, Assistant
Sybil Novinski Sutton, Rome Office Director

Spring 2000

Wayne Ambler, Program Director
Randy Irlbeck, Campus Director
Scott Crider, English
Laura Flusche, Art History
Peter Hatlie, History
Michael McShane, Philosophy
Lisa Mobus, Italian
Michael Terranova, Theology
Father James Conley, Chaplain
Jeff Mobus, Campus Manager
Sarah Dawson, Assistant
Dustin Gish, Assistant
Joe Weinpel, Assistant
Sybil Novinski Sutton, Rome Office Director

Fall 2000

Wayne Ambler, Dean, Italian
Seemee Ali, English
Beatrice De Magistris, Italian
Laura Flusche, Art History
Peter Hatlie, History
Michael McShane, Philosophy
Lisa Mobus, Italian
Michael Terranova, Theology
Father James Conley, Chaplain

Jeff Mobus, Campus Manager
Michael Severance, Campus Manager
Jon Bird, Assistant
Terence Landry, Assistant
Christine Randazzo, Assistant
Gwyneth Weigel, Assistant
Sybil Novinski Sutton, Rome Office Director

Spring 2001

Wayne Ambler, Dean, Italian
Seemee Ali, English
Bill Brownsberger, Theology
Beatrice De Magistris, Italian
Laura Flusche, Art History
Peter Hatlie, History
Michael McShane, Philosophy
Monsignor James Conley, Chaplain

Michael Severance, Campus Manager
Jon Bird, Assistant
Terence Landry, Assistant
Christine Randazzo, Assistant
Gwyneth Weigel, Assistant
Sybil Novinski Sutton, Rome Office Director

Fall 2001

Wayne Ambler, Dean, Italian
Bill Brownsberger, Theology
Beatrice De Magistris, Italian
Laura Flusche, Art History
Peter Hatlie, History
Glen Thurow, Philosophy
Sarah Thurow, English
Monsignor James Conley, Chaplain

Michael Severance, Campus Manager
Christine Randazzo, Coordinator
Terence Landry, Coordinator
Rachel Armour, Assistant
Allie Speier, Assistant
Luke Speier, Assistant
Rebecca Davies, Rome Office Director

Spring 2002

Wayne Ambler, Dean
Bill Brownsberger, Theology
Beatrice De Magistris, Italian
Laura Flusche, Art History
Peter Hatlie, History
Glen Thurow, Philosophy
Sarah Thurow, English
Monsignor James Conley, Chaplain
Michael Severance, Campus Manager
Terence Landry, Coordinator
Luke Speier, Coordinator
Rachel Armour, Assistant
Allie Speier, Assistant
Rebecca Davies, Rome Office Director

Fall 2002

Wayne Ambler, Dean
William Brownsberger, Theology
Beatrice De Magistris, Italian, Office Manager
Laura Flusche, Art History
Peter Hatlie, History
Glen Thurow, Philosophy
Sarah Thurow, English
Monsignor James Conley, Chaplain
Michael Severance, Rome Campus Coordinator
Luke Speier, Coordinator for Student Activities
Francis Bitterman, Assistant
Amy Wadle, Assistant
Rebecca Davies, Rome Office Director

Spring 2003

Alison Lytle, Senior Director
Peter Hatlie, History, Academic Director
William Brownsberger, Theology
Beatrice De Magistris, Italian, Office Manager
Laura Flusche, Art History
Glen Thurow, Philosophy
Sarah Thurow, English
Monsignor James Conley, Chaplain
Monsignor Thomas Fucinaro, Assistant Chaplain
Michael Severance, Rome Campus Director
Luke Speier, Coordinator for Student Activities
Francis Bitterman, Assistant
Katie McEwen, Assistant
Allison Speier, Assistant
Amy Wadle, Assistant
Fabio Cinalli, Facilities Manager
Rebecca Davies, Rome Office Director

Fall 2003

Alison Lytle, Senior Director
William Frank, Philosophy, Academic Director
Beatrice De Magistris, Italian, Office Manager
Laura Flusche, Art History
Therese Frank, Theology
Peter Hatlie, History
Gregory Roper, English
Father Mark Byrne, SOLT, Chaplain
Francis Bitterman, Student Life Coordinator
Anne Johnson, Assistant
Eleanor Paynter, Assistant
Jimmy Wheaton, Assistant
Fabio Cinalli, Facilities Manager
Rebecca Davies, Rome Office Director

Spring 2004

Alison Lytle, Senior Director
William Frank, Philosophy, Academic Director
Beatrice De Magistris, Italian, Office Manager
Laura Flusche, Art History
Therese Frank, Theology
Peter Hatlie, History
Gregory Roper, English
Father Mark Byrne, SOLT, Chaplain
Francis Bitterman, Student Life Coordinator
Anne Johnson, Assistant
Eleanor Paynter, Assistant
Jimmy Wheaton, Assistant
Fabio Cinalli, Facilities Manager
Rebecca Davies, Rome Office Director

Fall 2004

Alison Lytle, Senior Director
William Frank, Philosophy, Academic Director
Beatrice De Magistris, Italian, Office Manager
Laura Flusche, Art History
Therese Frank, Theology
Peter Hatlie, History
Gregory Roper, English
Father Mark Byrne, SOLT, Chaplain
Anne Johnson, Coordinator for Student Life
Angie Bleichrodt, Assistant
Patrick Boos, Assistant
Mike Maiella, Assistant
Fabio Cinalli, Facilities Manager
Rebecca Davies, Rome Office Director

Spring 2005

Alison Lytle, Senior Director
William Frank, Philosophy, Academic Director
Beatrice De Magistris, Italian, Office Manager
Laura Flusche, Art History
Therese Frank, Theology
Peter Hatlie, History
Gregory Roper, English
Father Mark Byrne, SOLT, Chaplain
Anne Johnson, Coordinator for Student Life
Angie Bleichrodt, Assistant
Patrick Boos, Assistant
Mike Maiella, Assistant
Fabio Cinalli, Facilities Manager
Rebecca Davies, Rome Office Director

Fall 2005

Alison Lytle, Senior Director
Peter Hatlie, History, Academic Director
Beatrice De Magistris, Italian, Office Manager
Laura Flusche, Art History
Douglas Hadley, Philosophy
Andrew Moran, English
Joseph Stibora, Theology
Monsignor Thomas Fucinaro, Chaplain
Fabio Cinalli, Facilities Manager
Angie Bleichrodt, Coordinator for Student Life
Mike Maiella, Coordinator for Student Life
Eric Singh, Assistant
Mary Anne Tosetto, Assistant
Rebecca Davies, Rome Office Director

Spring 2006

Alison Lytle, Senior Director
Peter Hatlie, History, Academic Director
Beatrice De Magistris, Italian, Office Manager
Laura Flusche, Art History
Douglas Hadley, Philosophy
Andrew Moran, English
Joseph Stibora, Theology
Monsignor Thomas Fucinaro, Chaplain
Fabio Cinalli, Facilities Manager
Angie Bleichrodt, Coordinator for Student Life
Mike Maiella, Coordinator for Student Life
Mary Anne Tosetto, Assistant
Rebecca Davies, Rome Office Director

Fall 2006

Alison Lytle, Senior Director
Peter Hatlie, History, Academic Director
Beatrice De Magistris, Italian, Office Manager
Laura Flusche, Art History
Douglas Hadley, Philosophy
Andrew Moran, English
Joseph Stibora, Theology
Monsignor Thomas Fucinaro, Chaplain
Kara Maggiore, Assistant
John Rhodes, Assistant
Renee Talamantez, Assistant
Shane Lungwitz, Night Watchman
Fabio Cinalli, Facilities Manager
Rebecca Davies, Rome Office Director

Spring 2007

Alison Lytle, Senior Director
Peter Hatlie, History, Academic Director
Beatrice De Magistris, Italian, Office Manager
Laura Flusche, Art History
Douglas Hadley, Philosophy
Andrew Moran, English
Joseph Stibora, Theology
Monsignor Thomas Fucinaro, Chaplain
Kara Maggiore, Assistant
Ryan Reedy, Assistant
John Rhodes, Assistant
Renee Talamantez, Assistant
Shane Lungwitz, Power Forward
Fabio Cinalli, Facilities Manager
Rebecca Davies, Rome Office Director

Fall 2007

Alison Lytle, Senior Director
Peter Hatlie, History, Academic Director
Beatrice De Magistris, Italian, Office Manager
Laura Flusche, Art History
Douglas Hadley, Philosophy
Gregory Roper, English
Joseph Stibora, Theology
Monsignor Thomas Fucinaro, Chaplain
Kara Maggiore, Assistant
Ryan Reedy, Assistant
John Rhodes, Assistant
Renee Talamantez, Assistant
Fabio Cinalli, Facilities Manager
J.T. Kennelly, Facilities Assistant
Rebecca Davies, Rome Office Director

Spring 2008

Alison Lytle, Senior Director
Peter Hatlie, History, Academic Director
Beatrice De Magistris, Italian, Office Manager
Laura Flusche, Art History
Douglas Hadley, Philosophy
Gregory Roper, English
Joseph Stibora, Theology
Monsignor Thomas Fucinaro, Chaplain
J.T. Kennelly, Facilities Assistant
Ellen Flannery, Assistant
Kara Maggiore, Assistant
Ryan Reedy, Assistant
Renee Talamantez, Assistant
Fabio Cinalli, Facilities Manager
J.T. Kennelly, Facilities Assistant
Rebecca Davies, Rome Office Director

Fall 2008

Peter Hatlie, Director and Academic Dean, History
Bradford Blue, Philosophy
Laura Flusche, Art History
Mark Lowery, Theology
Gregory Roper, English
Monsignor Thomas Fucinaro, Chaplain
Silvia De Simone, Office Manager
Francesca Ronci, Office Assistant
Steve Bird, Assistant
Jennifer Brown, Assistant
Elizabeth Malone, Assistant
Fabio Cinalli, Facilities Manager
Rebecca Davies, Rome Office Director

Spring 2009

Peter Hatlie, Director and Academic Dean, History
Bradford Blue, Philosophy
Laura Flusche, Art History
Gregory Roper, English
Father Jeffrey Steenson, Theology
Monsignor Thomas Fucinaro, Chaplain
Father Brady Williams, Assistant
Silvia De Simone, Office Manager
Francesca Ronci, Office Assistant
Steve Bird, Assistant
Jennifer Brown, Assistant
Elizabeth Malone, Assistant
Fabio Cinalli, Facilities Manager
Rebecca Davies, Rome Office Director

Fall 2009

Peter Hatlie, Director and Academic Dean, History
Bradford Blue, Philosophy
David Dawson Vazquez, Theology
Laura Flusche, Art History, Associate Academic Dean
Bernadette Waterman Ward, English
Monsignor Thomas Fucinaro, Chaplain
Father Brady Williams, Assistant
Silvia De Simone, Office Manager
Alessandra Morello, Office Assistant
Cindy Bird, Assistant
Steve Bird, Assistant
Jon Polce, Assistant
Mary Schultze, Assistant
Fabio Cinalli, Facilities Manager
Rebecca Davies, Rome Office Director

Spring 2010

Peter Hatlie, Director and Academic Dean, History
Bradford Blue, Philosophy
David Dawson Vazquez, Theology
Laura Flusche, Art History, Associate Academic Dean
Bernadette Waterman Ward, English
Monsignor Thomas Fucinaro, Chaplain
Father Brady Williams, Assistant Chalplain
Silvia De Simone, Office Manager
Alessandra Morello, Office Assistant
Cindy Bird, Assistant
Steve Bird, Assistant
Jon Polce, Assistant
Mary Schultze, Assistant
Fabio Cinalli, Facilities Manager
Rebecca Davies, Rome Office Director

Fall 2010

Peter Hatlie, Director and Academic Dean, History
Maeve Heaney, Theology
Elizabeth Lisot, Art History, Associate Academic Dean
Griffin Nelson, Philosophy
Bernadette Waterman Ward, English
Monsignor Thomas Fucinaro, Chaplain
Father David Brown, SJ, Assistant Chaplain
Ryan Reedy, Vice Director
Silvia De Simone, Office Manager
Alessandra Morello, Office Assistant
Mary Dougherty, Assistant
Jon Polce, Assistant
Ellen Reedy, Assistant
Fabio Cinalli, Facilities Manager
Rebecca Davies, Rome Office Director

Spring 2011

Peter Hatlie, Director and Academic Dean, History
Maeve Heaney, Theology
Elizabeth Lisot, Art History, Associate Academic Dean
Griffin Nelson, Philosophy
Bernadette Waterman Ward, English
Monsignor Thomas Fucinaro, Chaplain
Father David Brown, SJ, Assistant Chaplain
Ryan Reedy, Vice Director
Silvia De Simone, Office Manager
Alessandra Morello, Office Assistant
Mary Dougherty, Assistant
Hannah Langsfeld, Assistant
Jon Polce, Assistant
Ellen Reedy, Assistant
Fabio Cinalli, Facilities Manager
Rebecca Davies, Rome Office Director

Fall 2011

Peter Hatlie, Director and Academic Dean, History
Valeria Cupelli, Italian
Sister Catherine Joseph Droste, OP, Theology
Elizabeth Lisot, Art History
Griffin Nelson, Philosophy
Andrew Osborn, English
Ilaria Pezzola, Italian
Monsignor Thomas Fucinaro, Chaplain
Father David Brown, SJ, Assistant Chaplain
Ryan Reedy, Vice Director
Silvia De Simone, Office Manager
Alessandra Morello, Office Assistant
Ellen Reedy, Coordinator of Student Life
Sarah Ambler, Assistant
Peter Blute, Assistant
Joey Pustejovsky, Assistant
Fabio Cinalli, Facilities Manager
Rebecca Davies, Rome Office Director

Spring 2012

Peter Hatlie, Director and Academic Dean, History
Valeria Cupelli, Italian
Sister Catherine Joseph Droste, OP, Theology
Elizabeth Lisot, Art History
Griffin Nelson, Philosophy
Andrew Osborn, English
Ilaria Pezzola, Italian
Monsignor Thomas Fucinaro, Chaplain
Father David Brown, SJ, Assistant Chaplain
Ryan Reedy, Vice Director
Silvia De Simone, Office Manager
Alessandra Morello, Office Assistant
Ellen Reedy, Coordinator of Student Life
Sarah Ambler, Assistant
Peter Blute, Assistant
Joey Pustejovsky, Assistant
Fabio Cinalli, Facilities Manager
Rebecca Davies, Rome Office Director

Fall 2012

Peter Hatlie, Director and Academic Dean, History
Valeria Cupelli, Italian
Sister Catherine Joseph Droste, OP, Theology
Elizabeth Lisot, Art History
Griffin Nelson, Philosophy
Andrew Osborn, English
Ilaria Pezzola, Italian
Monsignor Thomas Fucinaro, Chaplain
Father David Brown, SJ, Assistant Chaplain
Ryan Reedy, Vice Director
Silvia De Simone, Office Manager
Alessandra Morello, Office Assistant
Ellen Reedy, Coordinator of Student Life
Sarah Ambler, Assistant
Peter Blute, Assistant
Anthony Seiler, Assistant
Fabio Cinalli, Facilities Manager
Rebecca Davies, Rome Office Director

Spring 2013

Peter Hatlie, Director and Academic Dean, History
Valeria Cupelli, Italian
Sister Catherine Joseph Droste OP, Theology
Elizabeth Lisot, Art History
Griffin Nelson, Philosophy
Andrew Osborn, English
Ilaria Pezzola, Italian
Monsignor Thomas Fucinaro, Chaplain
Father David Brown, SJ, Assistant Chaplain
Ryan Reedy, Vice Director
Silvia De Simone, Office Manager
Alessandra Morello, Office Assistant
Ellen Reedy, Coordinator of Student Life
Sarah Ambler, Assistant
Peter Blute, Assistant
Anthony Seiler, Assistant
Fabio Cinalli, Facilities Manager
Rebecca Davies, Rome Office Director

Fall 2013

Peter Hatlie, Vice-President, Dean and Director, History
Valeria Cupelli, Italian
Giovanni Freni, Art History
Christina Morganti, Italian
Andrew Osborn, English
Ilaria Pezzola, Italian
Marianne Siegmund, Theology
William Tullius, Philosophy
Monsignor Thomas Fucinaro, Chaplain
Father David Brown, SJ, Assistant Chaplain
Ryan Reedy, Rome Program Vice-Director
Silvia De Simone, Office Manager
Alessandra Morello, Office Assistant
Renee Davis, Assistant
Anthony Seiler, Assistant
Michael Tann, Assistant
Mary-Elizabeth Zabilski, Assistant
Fabio Cinalli, Facilities Manager
Rebecca Davies, Rome Office Director

Spring 2014

Peter Hatlie, Vice-President, Dean and Director, History
Valeria Cupelli, Italian
Giovanni Freni, Art History
Christina Morganti, Italian
Andrew Osborn, English
Ilaria Pezzola, Italian
Marianne Siegmund, Theology
William Tullius, Philosophy
Monsignor Thomas Fucinaro, Chaplain
Father David Brown, SJ, Assistant Chaplain
Ryan Reedy, Rome Program Vice-Director
Silvia De Simone, Office Manager
Alessandra Morello, Office Assistant
Renee Davis, Assistant
Anthony Seiler, Assistant
Michael Tann, Assistant
Mary-Elizabeth Zabilski, Assistant
Fabio Cinalli, Facilities Manager
Rebecca Davies, Rome Office Director

Fall 2014

Peter Hatlie, Vice-President, Dean and Director, History
Valeria Cupelli, Italian
Sister Catherine Joseph Droste, OP, Theology
Giovanni Freni, Art History
Andrew Moran, English
Christina Morganti, Italian
Ilaria Pezzola, Italian
William Tullius, Philosophy
Monsignor Thomas Fucinaro, Chaplain
Father David Brown, SJ, Assistant Chaplain
Ryan Reedy, Rome Program Vice-Director
Silvia De Simone, Office Manager
Alessandra Morello, Office Assistant
Vallery Bergez, Assistant
Ivanna Bond, Assistant
Joseph Hrbacek, Assistant
Michael Tann, Assistant
Fabio Cinalli, Facilities Manager
Rebecca Davies, Rome Office Director

Spring 2015

Peter Hatlie, Vice-President, Dean and Director, History
Valeria Cupelli, Italian
Sister Catherine Joseph Droste, OP, Theology
Giovanni Freni, Art History
Andrew Moran, English
Christina Morganti, Italian
Ilaria Pezzola, Italian
William Tullius, Philosophy
Monsignor Thomas Fucinaro, Chaplain
Father David Brown, SJ, Assistant Chaplain
Ryan Reedy, Rome Program Vice-Director
Silvia De Simone, Office Manager
Alessandra Morello, Office Assistant
Vallery Bergez, Assistant
Ivanna Bond, Assistant
Joseph Hrbacek, Assistant
Michael Tann, Assistant
Fabio Cinalli, Facilities Manager
Rebecca Davies, Rome Office Director

Fall 2015

Peter Hatlie, Vice-President, Dean and Director, History
Valeria Cupelli, Italian
Andrew Glicksman, Theology
Christopher Mirus, Philosophy
Andrew Moran, English
Christina Morganti, Italian
Elizabeth Robinson, Art History
Monsignor Thomas Fucinaro, Chaplain
Father David Brown, SJ, Assistant Chaplain
Ryan Reedy, Rome Program Vice-Director
Silvia De Simone, Office Manager
Alessandra Morello, Office Assistant
Vallery Bergez, Assistant
Ivanna Bond, Assistant
Joseph Hrbacek, Assistant
Michael Pitstick, Assistant
Fabio Cinalli, Facilities Manager
Rebecca Davies, Rome Office Director

Spring 2016

Peter Hatlie, Vice-President, Dean and Director, History
Valeria Cupelli, Italian
Andrew Glicksman, Theology
Christopher Mirus, Philosophy
Andrew Moran, English
Christina Morganti, Italian
Elizabeth Robinson, Art History
Monsignor Thomas Fucinaro, Chaplain
Father David Brown, SJ, Assistant Chaplain
Ryan Reedy, Rome Program Vice-Director
Silvia De Simone, Office Manager
Alessandra Morello, Office Assistant
Vallery Bergez, Assistant
Ivanna Bond, Assistant
Joseph Hrbacek, Assistant
Michael Pitstick, Assistant
Fabio Cinalli, Facilities Manager
Rebecca Davies, Rome Office Director

Fall 2016

Peter Hatlie, Vice-President, Dean and Director, History
Sara Abbate, Italian
Valeria Cupelli, Italian
Andrew Glicksman, Theology
Christopher Mirus, Philosophy
Andrew Moran, English
Christina Morganti, Italian
Elizabeth Robinson, Art History
Monsignor Thomas Fucinaro, Chaplain
Father David Brown, SJ, Assistant Chaplain
Ryan Reedy, Rome Program Vice-Director
Silvia De Simone, Office Manager
Alessandra Morello, Office Assistant
Ivanna Bond, Assistant
Keelin des Rosiers, Assistant
David Flynn, Assistant
Michael Pitstick, Assistant
Fabio Cinalli, Facilities Manager
Rebecca Davies, Rome Office Director

Spring 2017

Peter Hatlie, Vice-President, Dean and Director, History
Sara Abbate, Italian
Valeria Cupelli, Italian
Kathryn Davis, English
Andrew Glicksman, Theology
Christopher Mirus, Philosophy
Christina Morganti, Italian
Elizabeth Robinson, Art History
Monsignor Thomas Fucinaro, Chaplain
Father David Brown, SJ, Assistant Chaplain
Ryan Reedy, Rome Program Vice-Director
Silvia De Simone, Office Manager
Alessandra Morello, Office Assistant
Ivanna Bond, Assistant
Keelin des Rosiers, Assistant
David Flynn, Assistant
Michael Pitstick, Assistant
Fabio Cinalli, Facilities Manager
Rebecca Davies, Rome Office Director

Fall 2017

Peter Hatlie, Vice-President, Dean and Director, History
Sara Abbate, Italian
Valeria Cupelli, Italian
Kathryn Davis, English
Philip Gonzales, Philosophy
Christina Morganti, Italian
Father James Oberle, SS, Theology
Elizabeth Robinson, Art History
Monsignor Thomas Fucinaro, Chaplain
Father David Brown, SJ, Assistant Chaplain
Lucas Preble, Director Student Affairs
Silvia De Simone, Office Manager
Alessandra Morello, Office Assistant
Stephen Henderson, Assistant
Anna Hotard, Assistant
Rachel Parkey, Assistant
Fabio Cinalli, Facilities Manager
Rebecca Davies, Rome Office Director

Spring 2018

Peter Hatlie, Vice-President, Dean and Director, History
Sara Abbate, Italian
Valeria Cupelli, Italian
Kathryn Davis, English
Philip Gonzales, Philosophy
Christina Morganti, Italian
Father James Oberle, SS, Theology
Elizabeth Robinson, Art History
Monsignor Thomas Fucinaro, Chaplain
Father David Brown, SJ, Assistant Chaplain
Lucas Preble, Director Student Affairs
Silvia De Simone, Office Manager
Alessandra Morello, Office Assistant
Stephen Henderson, Assistant
Anna Hotard, Assistant
Rachel Parkey, Assistant
Fabio Cinalli, Facilities Manager
Rebecca Davies, Rome Office Director

Fall 2018

Peter Hatlie, Vice-President, Dean and Director, History
Sara Abbate, Italian
Scott Crider, English
Valeria Cupelli, Italian
David Dawson Vasquez, Theology
Philip Gonzales, Philosophy
Christina Morganti, Italian
Elizabeth Robinson, Art History, Assistant Dean
Monsignor Thomas Fucinaro, Chaplain
Father David Brown, SJ, Assistant Chaplain
Silvia De Simone, Office Manager
Alessandra Morello, Office Assistant
Benedetta Barbieri, Office Assistant
Ben Gibbs, Director, Student Affairs
Annie Gibbs, Director, Special Programs
Alina Chiriac, Services Manager
Vasile Chiriac, Services Assistant
Theresa Guin, Assistant
Stephen Henderson, Assistant
Fabio Cinalli, Facilities Manager
Rebecca Davies, Rome Office Director

Spring 2019

Peter Hatlie, Vice-President, Dean and Director, History
Sara Abbate, Italian
Scott Crider, English
Valeria Cupelli, Italian
Erica D'Amico, Art History
David Dawson Vasquez, Theology
Philip Gonzales, Philosophy
Christina Morganti, Italian
Monsignor Thomas Fucinaro, Chaplain
Father David Brown, SJ, Assistant Chaplain
Silvia De Simone, Office Manager
Alessandra Morello, Office Assistant
Benedetta Barbieri, Office Assistant
Ben Gibbs, Director, Student Affairs
Annie Gibbs, Director, Special Programs
Alina Chiriac, Services Manager
Vasile Chiriac, Services Assistant
Theresa Guin, Assistant
Stephen Henderson, Assistant
Fabio Cinalli, Facilities Manager
Rebecca Davies, Rome Office Director

Fall 2019

Peter Hatlie, Vice-President, Dean and Director, History
Sara Abbate, Italian
Scott Crider, English
Valeria Cupelli, Italian
Christina Morganti, Italian
Catherine Nolan, Philosophy
Elizabeth Robinson, Art History, Assistant Dean
Ron Rombs, Theology
Monsignor Thomas Fucinaro, Chaplain
Father David Brown, SJ, Assistant Chaplain
Silvia De Simone, Office Manager
Alessandra Morello, Office Assistant
Benedetta Barbieri, Office Assistant
Ben Gibbs, Director, Student Affairs
Annie Gibbs, Director, Special Programs
Alina Chiriac, Services Manager
Vasile Chiriac, Services Assistant
Joe Griesbauer, Assistant
Theresa Guin, Assistant
Fabio Cinalli, Facilities Manager
Rebecca Davies, Rome Office Director

Spring 2020

Peter Hatlie, Vice-President, Dean and Director, History
Sara Abbate, Italian
Scott Crider, English
Valeria Cupelli, Italian
Christina Morganti, Italian
Catherine Nolan, Philosophy
Elizabeth Robinson, Art History, Assistant Dean
Ron Rombs, Theology
Monsignor Thomas Fucinaro, Chaplain
Father David Brown, SJ, Assistant Chaplain
Silvia De Simone, Office Manager
Alessandra Morello, Office Assistant
Benedetta Barbieri, Office Assistant
Ben Gibbs, Director, Student Affairs
Annie Gibbs, Director, Special Programs
Alina Chiriac, Services Manager
Vasile Chiriac, Services Assistant
Joe Griesbauer, Assistant
Theresa Guin, Assistant
Fabio Cinalli, Facilities Manager
Rebecca Davies, Rome Office Director

ABOUT THE CONTRIBUTORS

In the order in which they appear in this volume.

Thomas Hibbs became the first alumnus president of the University of Dallas in 2019 after serving as the dean of the Honors College at Baylor University, chair of philosophy at Boston College, and tutor at Thomas Aquinas College. Author of more than thirty scholarly articles and more than one hundred reviews and articles on film, theater, art, and higher education, his most recent book, *Wagering on an Ironic God: Pascal on Philosophy and Faith*, was published by Baylor University Press in 2017.

Wayne Ambler's degrees are in political philosophy and classics, and he taught at the University of Dallas from 1979 through 2002. He and his family spent ten of these years on UD Rome Campuses, where he taught Western Civilization I and later served as academic director and, later, as dean. He then became the director of the Herbst Program of Humanities at the University of Colorado–Boulder. His scholarly work is mostly on Aristotle, Xenophon, and Plato.

As dean and director of the Rome Program, Peter Hatlie oversees every aspect of campus administration, including construction and facilities, finance and legal affairs, fundraising, and faculty and staff stewardship. As Professor of Classics, he has taught the Western Civilization I core class to thousands of students in a career spanning over twenty years, and he is also a recognized scholar of the early Byzantine period. His book *The Monks and Monasteries of Constantinople* (circa 350–850) was published by Cambridge University Press in 2007. A more recent edited volume, *People and Places of the Roman Past: An Educated Traveller's Guide* (ARC Humanities-Amsterdam University Press, 2019), is a visitor's companion to the history and culture of the Eternal City written by UD professors.

Michael Housewright, BA, drama, '95, itinerant wine gospel proselytizer and lifelong wine professional, is the importer of and chief advocate for Due Santi Wines. His photographs and award-winning video productions can be found in some of the world's leading wine industry publications, and his passion and dedication for UD's wine product have fostered growth around the country. A proud Fall 1992 Romer, he has lived in Italy on numerous occasions and has made yearly pilgrimages to Due Santi since 2012.

Gregory Roper returned to UD as associate professor of English in 2000 and taught on the Rome Program from 2003 to 2005 and from 2007 to 2009. He also directed the high school summer Shakespeare in Italy program from 2004 to 2017. A published scholar on Chaucer and the *Gawain*-poet, he is also the author of *The Writer's Workshop: Imitating Your Way to Better Writing*. In his 1984 UD senior yearbook, he claimed Assisi as his hometown.

Andrew Moran, an associate professor of English at UD, was a Fall 1988 Romer, the last semester to be instructed by Jim Fougerousse on where to find the best bars. He taught at Due Santi from 2005 to 2007 and from 2014 to 2016 and is now the director of the summer programs Shakespeare in Italy and Classical Education in Rome. The author of articles on Shakespeare, Ben Jonson, and Evelyn Waugh, he is currently writing a book on Shakespeare's comedies.

Lisa Fougerousse Mobus graduated from UD in 1990 with a BA in English and elementary education. She worked on the Rome campus for nine and a half years, first as a Rome assistant and then as an adjunct professor of Italian. She now lives in Vermont, teaching English at a public middle school.

Daniel Milligan only discovered in architecture school what a great gift it had been to be taught by Christian Norberg-Schulz during his Fall 1988 Rome Program. Now a practicing architect himself, he still draws on the lessons from his UD education. He and his wife, Kathy, along with her family, established the Uhl Family Scholarship so more students can attend the Rome Program.

Lyle Novinski is Professor Emeritus of Art and former chair of the Art Department at the University of Dallas. His interests as a working artist include a wide range of topics, including painting as a discipline, design and execution of liturgical spaces, and the history of sacred art. His many exhibits over the years have brought note to his work, with more than sixty installations in churches, including the windows of St. Rita's in Dallas and furnishings for the Neuhoff Chapel at SMU.

Due Santi at sunset.
Vasile Chiriac.

Vallery Bergez Hrbacek graduated with a BA in English and French in 2014 and worked on the Rome Campus for two years as a Rome assistant. She now lives in Dallas and works for a local pregnancy clinic called Birth Choice of Dallas.

UD Rome's Business Office manager, Silvia De Simone, graduated from the University of Naples in 1986 with a specialization in foreign languages, notably English and French. Mother of two children, her previous work experience involved administrative, translating, and marketing activities. She has also worked for an American pharmaceutical company, the American Consulate General in Naples, as well as the American Embassy in Rome. In July 2008, after dedicating some years to her family, she started to work for the University of Dallas.